of invasion **D-Day**

R. W. Thompson

ᗷB

PHOTO CREDITS:
Photographs for this book were specially selected from the following Archives: from left to right Page 2–3 US National Archives; 7 Imperial War Museum; 9 United Press International; 10 IWM; 11 IWM; 12 Ullstein; 14 US Army; 15 IWM/US Signal Corps/IWM; 18–19 IWM; 20–21 US Nat. Arch.; 22–23 US Army; 25 IWM; 31 UPI; 32 IWM; 33 Associated Press/US Army; 34 US Army; 35 IWM; 44–45 UPI; 47 Suddeutscher Verlag; 48 IWM; 50 Sado-Opera Mundi/Ullstein; 51 Sado-Opera Mundi; 53 Sado-Opera Mundi; 54 Bundesarchiv; 55 Sado-Opera Mundi; 57 Sado-Opera Mundi; 63 Sado-Opera Mundi; 65 Sado-Opera Mundi; 66–67 US Army; 68 US Army; 71 US Army; 74–75 US Navy; 75 US Navy; 76 US Army; 77 US Signal Corps/US Army; 78 IWM/US Army; 79 Sado-Opera Mundi; 81 IWM/US Coast Guard/US Navy/IWM; 82 US Nat. Arch; 83 US Coast Guard/US Army; 85 US Air Force; 87 US Coast Guard; 88 US Army/US Signal Corps; 89 US Army/IWM; 90–91 US Army; 93 US Army/Ullstein/US Army; 94–95 IWM; 96–97 UPI; 98 IWM; 98–99 IWM; 100–101 US Nat. Arch; 100 IWM; 101 IWM; 102 US Army; 103 US Nat. Arch/US Army; 104 IWM/Keystone; 105 UPI/Keystone; 106 US Army; 107 Keystone; 108 US Army; 109 US Army/US Nat. Arch/US Army; 110–111 UPI; 112 US Navy; 114–115 US Signal Corps; 116 US Army; 118 US Nat. Arch; 120–121 IWM; 122 IWM/Sado-Opera Mundi; 124 IWM; 125 IWM/Sado-Opera Mundi; 127 Sado-Opera Mundi; 130–131 IWM; 132–133 Ullstein; 133 Sado-Opera Mundi; 134 IWM/Popperfoto; 135 IWM; 137 IWM; 138 IWM; 139 IWM; 142 IWM; 143 IWM; 144 IWM; 144–145 UPI; 145 IWM/Ullstein; 146 IWM; 147 Sado-Opera Mundi; 149 IWM; 150–151 US Army; 154 US Coast Guard; 156–157 US Nat. Arch; 158 US Army.

ISBN 0-345-25887-8-250

Manufactured in the United States of America

First Edition: May 1968
Third Printing: April 1977

Editor-in-Chief: Barrie Pitt
Art Director: Peter Dunbar
Military Consultant: Sir Basil Liddell Hart
Picture Editor: Robert Hunt
Design Assistants: Gibson/Marsh, Philip Thompson, Trevor Wooldridge
Research Assistant: Yvonne Marsh
Cartographer: Richard Natkiel
Special Drawings: John Batchelor

Contents

The day of destiny

Introduction by Captain Sir Basil Liddell Hart

There is no more memorable day in recent history than D-Day in Normandy 1944 – and R W Thompson has written a memorable account to match it. He catches, and conveys, the atmosphere and the tension of June 6th. At the same time he produces out of the turmoil – its hazards, mishaps, and achievements – a remarkably clear picture of the course of operations and the factors affecting them. Despite the emotional intensity that he shows, and evidently feels, the picture never becomes blurred or its outlines distorted. It is not only a book but a deed.

The story opens with the situation in Britain at the beginning of spring 1944, and provides a graphically clear record of the manifold preparations for the coming Allied re-entry into Europe by way of Normandy, including the security precautions. Besides the British forces, there were three-quarters of a million from the United States at the start of the year, and that number was more than doubled by the end of May – so that the total had by then become eleven combat divisions, with more on the way. The American troops were mostly stationed in the south-west and west of the country, roughly from Southampton westward, while the British forces for the Normandy invasion were in the south-east, mainly in Hampshire and Sussex.

British uniforms were so rare in the south-west, apart from soldiers on home leave, that this part was ironically described by its inhabitants as 'occupied England', a point that Thompson does not mention. The description was usually applied jestingly, not bitterly, thanks to the good relations generally established between the American troops and the people of the areas where they had been stationed – a fact to which I can bear personal testimony, having spent most of February and March in visiting the spearhead divisions and their commanders in that region.

The prime reason for the separate lay-out was the trouble and confusion likely to arise if the British and American lines of supply and communication were to cross. It was a point often emphasised in the preparatory discussions, particularly by General Montgomery, who had now

been appointed to exercise overall command of the invading forces under General Eisenhower, who had been nominated as Supreme Commander. On the other hand, the palpably separate lay-out provided a pointer to the fact that the two-fold invasion was planned to come convergingly on the opposite stretch of coast, between the Cherbourg and Havre peninsulas. Hitler, actually, was the first to deduce the strategic significance of this lay-out, and various supporting signs. But, fortunately for the Allies, the German military Commander-in-Chief in the West, Field-Marshal von Rundstedt, ignored them because of his conviction that the correct course for the Allies was to make their landing in the narrow straits of the English Channel, the sector nearest to Germany.

After an illuminating account of the dissensions within the enemy command – between Rundstedt and Rommel as well as between Hitler and Rundstedt – Thompson comes to D-Day itself, of which he provides a most vivid and penetrating account. He gives priority, and predominance, in his story to the airborne operations on either flank, which initiated the cross-Channel attack; but although his account of the seaborne landings is relatively brief it brings out most of the key points – and with remarkable conciseness. Indeed, the outstanding quality of the book as a whole is the able way it marshals the salient facts while bringing out, and impressing on the reader, the emotional depths behind the facts.

Embattled isle

No visitor to Britain in the early Spring of 1944 – and there were some two million visitors – could have failed to observe the sources of the Island's strength. The evidences of her Maritime Power, which had enabled her through the centuries, not only to repel the threats of Philip of Spain, Napoleon of France and Hitler of Germany, but also to found an Empire covering one-fourth of the surface of the earth, lay not only in the seas around her, patrolled constantly by big and little ships of war, in the hundreds of ports seething with shipping in astonishing variety, in the numerous 'hards', or ramps, enabling her to launch and land craft of many kinds from beaches and estuaries, in the shipyards bristling with the naked struts and ribs and stays of a great multitude of vessels under construction, and all the immense activities of her coasts, but also deep inland, in her resources in coal, iron and steel, in heavy and light industry, above all in the pre-occupation of the people. Ships were not confined to shipyards, they grew in narrow streets, in alleyways, prefabricated in scores of workshops. Not only ships and craft, but 'things to float' rose under the hammers of tens of thousands of workmen. Shipbuilding, it almost seemed, had become a 'cottage industry', and children homing from their schools stopped to stare at the welders and the riveters, fascinated by the steel skeletons taking shape outside their doors.

Even many of the principal activities of the army had a snatch of the sea. Naval and military men worked together in numerous 'combined' tasks under Major-General Hobart.

Churchill and Sherman tanks, after much trial and error, were adapted to deal with the scores of obstacles to be faced in the assault on the Normandy beaches. The 79th Armoured Division grew to 1,000 armoured vehicles, destined to lead the assault.

The demand for crews for the many thousands of specialised vehicles put a great strain on manpower already strained to the limits, for the crews must be men of skill, courage and resource, and of strong character, and it seemed that the combined demands of the mass of specialised land and sea vehicles, as well as the Naval, Military and Marine Commandos, might strip the conventional services of many of their best personnel. While Hobart was training crews for his amphibians the Navy was training crews for its great host of landing craft, tank landing craft, assault landing craft, craft mounted with batteries of rockets which could devastate whole villages with a salvo and which seared the decks of their parent vessels with flame, landing craft adapted for special survey work, even small submarines known as X-craft to lay off the enemy shore in the shallows, all had to be manned with brave and expert crews, and many were involved in constant action against the enemy through their periods of training.

The Allied Supreme Command.
Left to Right: Lieutenant General Omar N. Bradley; Admiral Sir Bertram Ramsay; Air Chief Marshal Sir Arthur Tedder; General Dwight D.Eisenhower; General Sir Bernard Montgomery; Air Chief Marshal Sir Trafford Leigh Mallory; Lieutenant General Walter Bedell Smith

It is important, I believe, to underline the remarkable integration of the services in combining sea and land power into a single potent weapon which, in fact, was the 'tin-opener' into Normandy.

In the early Spring of 1944, most of these activities were reaching their peaks. An extra month, so desperately needed, so grudgingly gained, before 'D day', was revealed as indispensable to success. Without that extra month the great artificial harbours upon which success in sustaining the battle for Normandy must depend, could not have been ready, and the assault, however well it might fare, would have been in vain. These great artificial harbours known as 'Mulberries' and protected by breakwaters known as 'Gooseberries' were of singular complexity, comprising roadways known as 'Whale' units, caissons of steel and concrete, known as 'Phoenix' units, 'Beetles', and a whole 'menagerie' of accessories. A total of 146 Phoenix caissons was needed, ranging from 10 of the smallest size, each of 1,672 tons through six sizes to the 60 largest, each of 6,044 tons. 600,000 tons of concrete, 31,000 tons of steel, and 1,500,000 yards of steel shuttering were consumed in their construction. The eight dry docks and two wet docks made available with great difficulty had to be supplemented by twelve great holes excavated on Thames side below water level, and leaving a barrier of earth between them and the river. The earth barriers would be breached when the caissons were ready to float out into the stream. 20,000 men worked overtime for months while the pumps continuously fought the encroaching waters.

But to construct these strange objects, completely baffling to enemy air reconnaissance, was not enough. They had not only to float, but to sink fast in varying depths according to their sizes. After much trial and error the sinking time of the largest caissons was reduced from $1\frac{1}{2}$ hours to 22 minutes. Each 'Phoenix' was also a 'kind of ship', provided with quarters for a crew, and mounting two Bofors guns with 20 tons of ammunition. They could not sail under their own steam, however, and when they were completed it was found that the towing fixture gear was inadequate. Teams of riggers in Chatham Naval dockyard worked day and night in the last weeks to make them secure for the tugs.

The safe passage of 146 of these 'monsters' was only one of many towing problems, demanding a great fleet of tugs to deliver them safely across the Channel and manoeuvre them into

The Vital Key: Pre-fabricated Harbours.
146 of these monsters – the Phoenix
Caissons – had to be towed across the
Channel and sunk exactly in position.
Below left: Segments of pier for
off-loading. *Below:* Period of trial:
fitting the pieces together

their exact positions based on the
gradient of the sea bottom. There
were also, as an item, some 70 old ships,
many of them old warships with proud
names, to be towed out and sunk to
form the 'Gooseberries'.

There were in all more than 3,000
small craft, lighters and barges,
manned by 15,000 men, involved in the
'artificial harbour project', which was
going into service direct from the
drawing boards. As an item the pier
heads, each of 1,000 tons of steel, were
needed to anchor on the beaches, and
the mass of material behind them, the
thousands of yards of 'floating bridge'
roadway, had to rise and fall 20 feet
with the tide, all within the 24,000 feet
of breakwater provided by the sunken
block ships.

By such means, Admiral Ramsay, commanding the Allied Naval Forces, hoped to build a stable bridge to France, and to achieve a delivery of up to 12,000 tons of supplies each day to the 33 divisions to be fed with food and ammunition at the peak of the Mulberry service from the shores of Arromanches. Meanwhile 'Pluto', the pipe-line-under-the-ocean, was designed to carry oil fuel to Cherbourg, and later to more accessible points on the French and Belgian coasts.

To describe these activities as a microcosm of the tasks involved in launching a successful assault across the Channel against a sixty-mile wide stretch of the 'Atlantic Wall' is perhaps an under-statement, but it is not a serious under-statement. Rear Admiral W. G. Tennant, who had achieved great things as a Captain on the beaches of Dunkirk, saw the 'Mulberry' project through with a Naval Staff of 500 officers and 10,000 men apart from the large labour force involved. The enterprise tied in with a remarkable galaxy of organisations bearing 'mystical' code names which, from those days, wrote themselves temporarily into the language so that each service developed a form of jargon. 'Buco' stood for the build-up control organisation, 'Turco' for the turn-round control, 'Corep' for the

Outposts of the Atlantic Wall : Rommel inspects his new responsibilities, before D-Day

control repair, 'Cotug' for the control tug organisation, and these bred many lesser brands of initials like a warren of rabbits.

But all these major projects and activities, indeed all the activities taking place in the Island, covering all the known facets of war, and many previously unknown, all the intricate plans, the miracles of production, transport, assembly, training and organisation, were dependent in great measure for success upon the activities of a very small and select band of men combining qualities of great daring with extraordinary patience and ingenuity. Upon the accuracy of the information these men provided would depend success or failure. Air photography, valuable as it was, was not enough. It was essential to know, for example, the exact geological composition of the beaches, the rocks, the runs-in, over sixty miles of enemy held coast subject to constant vigilance and incessant enemy activity.

It was of great help to the engineers who would go in ahead of the assault troops, often under water, to know exactly the nature of the many lethal obstacles the enemy constantly devised and sowed in swathes in the sea approaches. These included massive 'Tetrahydra', 'Belgian Gates', and 'Element C'. To know them was to disarm them, and to discover these things, and many others, to explore the estuaries of the Orne, the Vire and lesser streams, to neutralise enemy

2

mining of locks that would block the entry of Allied barges and lighters, was the rôle of small tight groups of young men of a physical and nervous calibre to withstand extremes of temperature, to be still almost under the feet of the enemy, to endure many lonely vigils, and with no resources other than the human spirit to sustain them. Many such men there had been since the days of Dunkirk, and their services were incomparable. For these war provided the opportunities men often seek in vain in peace. Night after moonless-night in summer and winter they left the shores of the Island, sneaking out from the quiet estuary of the Hamble, from the Solent, and homing back to the green grass domes of the old Forts Brockhurst and Gomer with their 'spoils of war'. Towed in their landing craft adapted for survey work behind Naval ML's, they left their parent craft to propel themselves ashore in folboats or to take at once to the water, using the apparatus for under-water swimming. Thus they moved in the shallows through lethal forests, sometimes laying charges, more often removing those of the enemy, making mental notes from which to produce accurate diagrams, noting tidal conditions, changes of the sea bed, and collecting samples from scores of points for the experts to consider. A sudden doubt in an expert mind would send a party at once back to any given point to check, for on such things must depend the movement of armour out of the sea.

In the last few months before 'D day' security demanded the severe limitation of civilian movement. The coastal belt of the Island was frozen ten miles deep from the Wash southward and westward to Land's End, and from Dunbar to Arbroath in Scotland. Innumerable prohibited areas, including forests such as Sherwood, had become ammunition dumps, and mazes of air-fields, camps and vehicle parks, still further confined the civilian population. Millions of men and women lived within the wire against the sea, millions more inhabited the inner cage, no less restricted than the sealed-off troops. In fact civilian life had almost ceased to exist, yet it was essential that many of its functions should be preserved.

On the 10th March all movement, communications and mail, became subject to strict control, but even without control the immense weight of military traffic on roads and railways made civilian movement next to impossible. Few had travelled in comfort for at least three years. Few attempted to go anywhere, although to do so was an immense relief. National Registration and rationing of all food and essential commodities had long since reduced the inhabitants to 'statistics'. Apart from doctors, others on essential business and a few limited privileged groups, no civilian had the means to use the roads other than by bicycle or on foot. The roads, in any case, had become death-traps over which fast convoys had begun to roar at breakneck speeds in endless streams, so that houses bordering the narrow streets of towns and villages shuddered through all the hours of day and night to the thunder of wheels.

On the 6th April, all military leave was stopped, and the last slack in the censorship of mails and communications of all kinds was drawn tight. The War Cabinet, gravely troubled, but unable to refuse the reasonable wishes of the Supreme Commander, imposed severe restrictions on diplomatic privileges, held up diplomatic bags, and watched embassies. It was difficult, if not impossible, to grade foreign embassies in a security sense, for the most loyal of allies might harbour enemies or fools. It was simpler to watch all equally rather than to attempt to watch this man or that man more than the next.

Indeed, in the Spring of 1944, the mood of the British people was undergoing a subtle change, compounded of unease and relief in roughly equal proportions. They were glad of the outward and visible signs of the physical aid they so sorely needed; they feared the unspoken implications of the huge 'invasion' which changed the nature of the Island, it might be forever. They were closer in a hundred ways to the refugees, the Europeans and the Scandinavians, in their midst, fighting at their side on similar 'shoe-strings' for the return to their Continent, than to the men of the New World with their alien habits and customs, their wealth of food, cloth-

ing, money, and with their eyes focused on a different vision. Perhaps it was easier for Churchill with his American blood to know them as 'cousins', to accept the inevitable passing of the precious sovereignty of Britain into hands that he did not regard as alien.

If indeed Britain had admitted a Trojan Horse within her gates, it was none the less certain that the hordes of troops pouring in from it were animated by the best possible intentions, including the very natural desire to return to their own land at the earliest possible moment. Each

British uniforms were so rare from Dorset down to Cornwall, apart from soldiers on home leave, that this part of the country was ironically described by its inhabitants as 'Occupied England'. *Left:* U.S. Armoured Unit, with pet crow, cheerfully await embarkation, frequently postponed. *Below left:* U.S. 4th Division marches through Torquay. *Upper right:* Approach to the docks. *Lower right:* Into the 'seal-off' area. *Below:* Lighter moments

man had been well briefed on some of the outstanding eccentricities of the British people, and was 'armed' with a booklet designed to aid him in avoiding treading too heavily upon the 'long toes' of the Islanders.

There were three quarters of a million members of the United States Forces in Britain on the 1st January, 1944, and new arrivals swelled the number to over one and one half million in the following five months. They brought with them an immense variety of weapons, ammunition and equipment, food and transport, and at a build-up rate of 750,000 tons of supplies a month. All these men and materials had to be channelled through 'their own' ports to the areas assigned to them. It had been fully understood by Cossac, and his American aides, at an early date, and was constantly emphasised by General Montgomery in the later stages, that it would be disastrous to permit the lines of supply and communication of the Allied armies to cross. Methods of organisation and administration, as well as equipment and supplies, were too diverse to blend.

The fact of two very large armies and all their services and stores based upon the same small and overcrowded Island, preparing to sail on the same day to take part in the same assault, and yet to be kept severely apart, posed problems of the utmost intricacy. Warehouses swiftly overflowed, and supplies were camouflaged all along the routes to the embarkation areas.

In the main the Americans occupied the west and south western coastal belt, their huts and tented camps dotting Cornwall, Devon and Dorset, with their supply and service 'tails' stretching far back into the Midlands. Hundreds of pieces of private property, farmlands and whole villages had been taken over in the face of fearsome legal difficulties, and even so the areas suitable for intensive assault training were barely adequate. For the US Airborne Forces, marshalling areas had been set aside north-west and north-east of London, Glider Troops in the West-Midlands, the 101st Division between Newbury and Exeter, the 82nd Division in the east.

The British and Canadian Forces were assembling in the south, basing themselves mainly upon the Hampshire and Sussex coasts, while the 'armies' of men and women to serve the Armies grew alarmingly. Gordon Harrison records that 54,000 men, 'including the temporary housekeeping services of the entire 5th Armoured Division, were required to establish and maintain installations for mounting the Seaborne Assault Forces alone, and to perform services necessary to make them ready for sailing'. More than 4,500 cooks were trained to cook for them in the first three months of the year, and more than 3,800 trucks moved their supplies.

On another level the Generals commanding the assault were fighting to keep down the vehicles to a maximum of 2,500 per Assault Division against the minimum estimates of 3,000.

The most meticulous planning of detail was necessary to ensure that all this mass of men, vehicles and shipping should come together at the right places at the right times, and with all that they would need, organised in the right order behind them. The last things in would be the first things out, and the supply lines had to be organised accordingly. At the same time the concentrations of men and shipping had to be camouflaged as much as possible from the enemy, and the innumerable activities of warfare slanted always to give a false impression of the target. The smoke of many fires rose from scores of dummy camps, while diversionary sorties in the Channel and far to the north were the constant pre-occupations of Naval and Air Forces. Some sections of a 'Mulberry' were sunk off Dungeness opposite Bordeaux to mislead the enemy. Extensive mine-laying operations bore a curious pattern from the Southern Baltic, between Sweden and Denmark, and down to the Pas de Calais, and air attacks against U-boats off the Norwegian coasts were designed to feed the fears of the enemy that an assault might be expected in that quarter. From Milford Haven to Harwich the southern ports of Britain were crammed with invasion shipping, and this led to an enormous concentration of ships of every conceivable kind in the northern and north-eastern ports. The 'look' of the Island, and the patterns of its actions could be read to mean an assault against almost anywhere. Carefully planted stories amongst elements of the Resistance Forces from Norway through Holland and France still further misled the enemy.

Intensive training for the 'Day' took place on land, sea and sky side by side with the 'live' operations of war. Brigades were landed with live ammunition under covering fire on the shores of Suffolk, North and South Devon and Dorset, as tens of thousands of Americans, Canadians and British rehearsed the ordeals they must face, and the crews of the landing craft learned to beach and unbeach their craft. In the more rugged parts of Scotland, Commando troops brought themselves to the peak of training, nearly all of them blooded in a score of assaults.

In September, 1943, the US Lt-Col Paul Thompson had established a training area on the perfect sweep of sandy beach between the Headlands of Morte and Baggy on the North Devon coast, and many hundreds of Americans owe their lives to his ingenuity, his ability to learn as well as to teach, and to imagine almost every possibility. From January to May, 1944, Lt-Col Thompson put all the Regiments of the US 29th Division and 4th Division, the 16th Infantry Regiment of the 1st Division, and elements of the 101st Airborne, through courses approximating to the realities of war.

Coils of barbed wire snaked out of the sandy draws of the combe, mines and bombs erupted in spouts of black smoke, flame and sand, and thousands of men leapt from their assault craft, up and over the beaches to the violent music of war. The authentic din of battle was there, but the leading actor did not attend rehearsals. Men did not choke and drown in their own blood, gaps did not open to leave men 'naked and alone', spattered with the entrails, blood and brains of their friends, nor did flying limbs and fragments torn from the bowels of men smite survivors haphazard, as though the world had

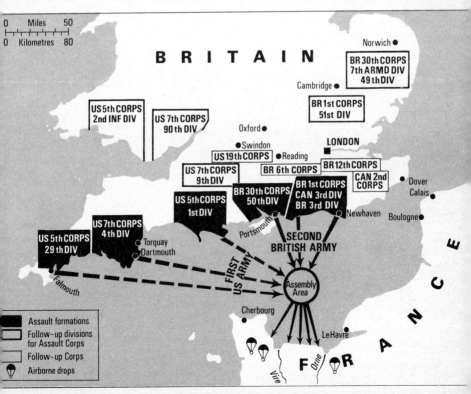

British assault troops rehearse the crucial moment

become suddenly the playground of some hideous poltergeists. Nor were the coils of wire littered with the obscene offal of war.

It was exciting; it was the best that could be devised, but the indescribable tension when the ramps go down was lacking. Only the 'Day' would produce the reality.

On the 26th April, the invasion forces for the assault were finally sealed in their embarkation areas.

Two days after the sealing the worst tragedy of training overtook the Infantry Landing Ships and men of part of the American Force U, exercising in the Channel in one of the two final assault rehearsals, code named, 'Tiger' and 'Fabius'. Two German E boat flotillas swooped in to sink two tank landing ships and damage a third. It is known that 749 men, predominantly engineer troops, lost their lives.

Perhaps no other incident reflected so grimly the shortage of assault shipping, for the Supreme Commander at once reported to the Combined Chiefs of Staff that the loss of the LST's had reduced the reserve 'to nothing'.

The 'D day' problem involved the pre-loading of 185,000 men and 20,000 vehicles in the initial assault lift, and thereafter the maintenance of a steady flow of men, equipment and stores to the beaches. These would be carried in 4,200 landing ships and craft, supported by 1,200 merchant ships and ancillary vessels, and with 1,200 warships, including 7 battleships and 23 cruisers. In the wake of this vast armada all the strange floating shapes of concrete and steel of the 'Mulberries' would lollop through the waters towed by a fleet of 100 tugs and ferries. Beach organisations would be set up ready to meet them, and trained crews would begin the complex task of erection. Frogmen and engineers working in the shallows would clear the forests of obstacles, and dismantle heavily mined contraptions of angle iron and steel.

Through the hours of darkness before the dawn the airborne vanguard, nearly 20,000 strong, would be carried in 1,087 transport aircraft and gliders

to their dropping zones behind the beaches. 10,000 aircraft would add to the immense weight of Naval fire power, which itself would be the heavy orchestra behind the rocket batteries and Bofors of the support landing craft, and the guns of tanks and artillery firing from their landing craft on the run in.

The 'Neptune' plan, covering every phase of the assault, except the air, made a printed book foolscap size three inches thick.

On the 26th April, Admiral Sir Bertram Ramsay, Commander-in-Chief, Naval Forces, moved into his advanced Headquarters at Southwick House, Portsmouth, and the five divisions chosen to assault the five main Normandy beaches in the Bay of Seine, moved into their embarkation areas with all their specialised assault troops, armour and ancillaries.

Each assaulting force bore the initial letter of the code-name given to the beach it would assault. The Western Force, U for 'Utah', the US 4th Infantry Division of VII Corps of the US 1st Army, spearheaded by 8 RCT concentrated upon Torbay, Brixham,

Dartmouth and Salcombe, would assault the Cherbourg Peninsula northwest of the Vire river on the extreme right flank. Force O for 'Omaha', the US 1st Infantry Division of V Corps of the US 1st Army, spearheaded by 16 RCT, would assault east of the Vire, concentrated upon Weymouth, Portland and Poole. The follow-up Force B, the US 29th Infantry Division, spearheaded by 116 RCT and with two battalions of US Rangers on its right, would assault on the right of the 1st Division, concentrated upon Plymouth, Falmouth, Helford River and Fowey. Behind them the Divisions for the build-up concentrated upon Bristol Channel ports.

In the assault the US 1st Army would be commanded by General Omar Bradley, until the arrival of the US 3rd Army commanded by Lieut-General George S. Patton, when Bradley would assume command of the US 12th Army Group.

The Eastern Force, G for 'Gold', spearheaded by the British 50th Division of the 30th Corps of the British 2nd Army, with 47 Commando strengthening its right, would assault

19

Arromanches, east of Port en Bessin, concentrated upon Southampton. Force J for 'Juno', concentrated upon Southampton, the Solent and Spithead, was spearheaded by the Canadian 3rd Division of the 1st Corps of the British 2nd Army, and would assault astride the Seulles river between La Rivière and Courselles sur Mer. Force S for 'Sword', concentrated upon Portsmouth, Newhaven and Shoreham, was spearheaded by the 3rd British Infantry Division of the 1st Corps of the British 2nd Army, and with the 1st and 4th SS Brigades on the right, and the 4th Commando on the left, would assault the beaches

Every day The Day came nearer

covering Douvres and Ouistreham. The follow-up Force L, the 7th Armoured Division of the 30th Corps, concentrated upon Harwich and the Nore, and would assault behind the 50th Division. The build-up divisions concentrated upon Thames ports.

The flails and specialised armour of Hobart's 79th Armoured Division would be at the service of the British and Canadians, but were refused by General Bradley. DD 'swimming' tanks would be supporting the entire assault.

The British 2nd Army was commanded by Lieut-General Miles Dempsey. The Canadian 1st Army, commanded by Lieut-General Crerar, would follow. The 21st Army Group,

commanded by General Sir Bernard Montgomery, Ground Force Commander for the assault and the Battle for Normandy, commanded the Allied armies.

Thus on the 26th April, the first rumblings of the great avalanche in its initial heave could be felt in every corner of the British Isles. At that time neither 'D day' nor 'H hour' had been fixed. The last arguments on time and tide, phases of the moon, even daylight or dark, had not been thrashed out to a final conclusion. Nevertheless, none doubted, however little 'in the know', that the hour was drawing near, that it could not be long delayed, that it seemed, in an eerie way, almost 'out of the hands of men', gathering its own momentum.

'Sooner or later', General Wavell had said, 'the time will come when Private Snodgrass must advance straight to his front'.

The hour was at hand.

The British and US Air Force Chiefs would have dissented from Wavell's view. They believed that they would win alone, without help on land or sea.

Embarkation for invasion

Pre D-Day airpower

The importance of air power in particular relation to the success or failure of 'Overlord' was fully realised in the Summer of 1943. The Combined Bomber offensive, authorised at Casablanca in January, designed to destroy the enemy economy and to undermine the morale of the German people, had not, at first sight, brought satisfactory results. In July, Cossac revealed his disquiet:

'The most significant feature of the German Air Force in Western Europe is the steady increase in its fighter strength which, unless checked and reduced, may reach such formidable proportions as to render an amphibious assault out of the question. Above all, therefore, an overall reduction in the strength of the German fighter force between now and the time for surface assault is essential.... This condition, above all others, will dictate whether amphibious assault can or cannot be successfully launched on any given date'.

A month earlier it had been noted on a higher level that unless the fighter strength of the enemy could be broken 'it may become literally impossible to carry out the destruction planned'. A new plan was drafted, Operation 'Pointblank', raising the reduction of the German fighter strength to the first priority while retaining the ultimate object of the bomber offensive.

These conclusions, with their notes of pessimism, were not shared by the bomber commanders, and were echoes of a new problem of immense significance. Air power, and particularly the bomber, had introduced a new dimension into warfare. Despite results, which were at best inconclusive, and the continued growth of enemy fighter strength, the Commanders of the Allied Strategic Air Forces had reached the conclusion that they controlled the decisive instrument; that they could achieve victory alone. General Spaatz, commanding the United States Strategic Air Force (USSTAF), believed simply that 'Overlord' was unnecessary. Air Chief Marshal Harris, his British opposite number, agreed with him. General Arnold, the representative of the US Air arm on the Joint Chiefs of Staff, had reached a similar conclusion. None of these commanders 'objected' to 'Overlord', or resented its demands upon their forces. They believed simply that if they continued with their bombing strategy the demands would be met.

Nazi Germany was being dissected, and destroyed behind its armies. The vast concentrations of heavy industry in the Ruhr and Saar valleys, coal, oil, synthetic fuels, ball bearings, roads, railways, cities and hamlets were all being steadily reduced to rubble at the whim of this man or that. The bomber chiefs were agreed on their mission, but not on their choices of targets. Oil, General Spaatz believed, was the essential upon which a modern nation at war must depend. Ball bearings, said another. Communications and morale, yet others.

These beliefs made the commanders of the strategic bomber forces careless of the tactical demands of armies. Strategically, they declared, the bomber is winning the war. To divert the bomber from its strategic mission was old fashioned and short-sighted. The German armies in the field, immensely powerful as they were, were nevertheless powerless to prevent the utter destruction of the homeland and people it was their rôle and purpose to defend.

Meanwhile, on the very highest levels there were forebodings of a very grave nature. Early in 1943, air photography and espionage had produced physical evidence of the enemy progress in the development and manufacture of rockets and pilotless aircraft capable of carrying warheads of high explosive distances of 150 miles plus. Such weapons might prove devastating in a high degree, and posed new problems of defence. In addition, the terrible secret of atomic progress engendered fears of enemy achievement in that field.

The odds were new and had to be considered urgently in the context of survival in a fight to the finish against an enemy who, it could be predicted, would stop at nothing. Never was the calm light of reason more necessary to mankind; seldom has it been less in evidence.

The bomber commanders, confident in their power, accepted an urgent mission to add the destruction of rocket and 'flying bomb' sites and bases to their commitments, and on 17th August, Air Chief Marshal Harris opened the attack with 571 heavy bombers on the enemy rocket base at Peenemünde. Finally, bombed out of Peenemünde, the German rocket experts under General Dornberger, moved into 'factories' deep in the Harz mountains, and continued their production on a reduced scale, while the 'ski-sites' for launching their pilotless aircraft grew in numbers, demanding constant vigilance and hammering from the air.

Despite successes it seemed that the Allies were faced with a grim race against time, even up to the end of March 1944. It was by then known that the enemy had improvised some form of modified launching site, very easily

Lieutenant General Frederick Morgan (COSSAC; Chief of Staff to the Supreme Allied Commander)

hidden from view. Many of these were suspected to exist in the Pas de Calais and the Cherbourg Peninsula, but the heavy and varied demands on the entire Allied air strength as 'Overlord' approached its hour, made it difficult to press consistent attacks.

The army commanders were at no time inclined to underestimate the gravity of the threat, and in early December Cossac had made an assessment. The immediate decision was to 'leave things as they were', but it was not until the 28th March that Eisenhower, emerging from 'a sea of troubles', reported that the 'Secret Weapon' attack 'would not preclude the launching of the assault from the south coast ports as now planned, and that the probable incidence of casualties does not make it necessary to attempt to move the assault forces west of Southampton'.

The problem of attempting to move the launching of the assault from one part of the coast to another was a greater hazard than the threat of the V1's and V2's on London and the south coast ports. The chance of massive enemy interference had to be taken.

The attitude of the 'Bomber Barons' made it inevitable that a serious command crisis would follow upon the appointment of a Supreme Commander for 'Overlord'. General Eisenhower was not slow to point out that, 'The strategic air arm is almost the only weapon at the disposal of the Supreme Commander for influencing the general course of action, particularly during the assault phase'.

This is a simple statement of fact, and no Supreme Commander worth his salt could have accepted the attitude of the Strategic Air Force Commanders, and abrogated his right to command. Without the command of the air forces in his hands the Supreme Commander would be reduced to a cypher, a mere pusher of the button, afterwards to sit back, certainly for days, possibly for weeks, with no real prospect of influencing the battle. In this context Eisenhower's statement to Churchill on the 3rd March that he would 'simply have to go home,' and his subsequent memo to Washington, dated 22nd March, 'unless the matter is settled at once I will request relief from this command,' lose all trace of petulance.

The fact was (and is) that the Supreme Commander in his fight with the Strategic Air Force Commanders in 1944, and to a great extent with the British Prime Minister and the Chiefs of Staff, emphasised the obvious truth that air, sea and land forces had become the three prongs of a single weapon. A Supreme Commander must command them all, and in submitting each service must lose some part of its separate identity.

In fact the demands of 'Overlord' and 'Pointblank', the Combined Bomber Offensive, were certainly not mutually exclusive or incompatible. The Supreme Commander had made it clear that in seeking command of the air forces he had not the smallest intention of interfering with, for example, Coastal Command. He had no quarrel with the strategic aims pursued by the bomber commanders – as far as they went, but he and his staff must have the right to state and to press their views on the use of air power in direct relation to 'Overlord', and to control it, at least, in the assault stages, and now, urgently, in the last ninety days.

Coincidentally, therefore, with the rather confused command arguments, an argument raged on the best way to serve 'Overlord' from the air. The Deputy Supreme Commander, Air Chief Marshal Sir Arthur Tedder, became the champion and chief exponent of what was known as 'The Transportation Plan' against General Spaatz, the champion and chief spokesman of 'The Oil Plan'. The argument, at times bitter, carried also grave political implications, and was pursued in an atmosphere of 'tense anxiety' through February and March into April.

All these difficulties were resolved by the middle of April largely by the efforts of two of the most experienced airmen in the world, both of whom happened to be men of outstanding character and ability, Air Chief Marshal Sir Charles Portal, a member of the Chiefs of Staff, and Tedder, Eisenhower's Deputy Supreme Commander.

Briefly, the 'Transportation Plan' aimed at the disruption of the enemy communications, the destruction of railways, locomotives, marshalling yards, repair and maintenance facilities, roads and bridges, and the prevention of enemy reserves reaching the battlefield. This, in General Eisenhower's view, was 'The greatest contribution he could imagine,' to the success of 'Overlord', and Tedder was his worthy champion.

Some idea of the feeling generated by this argument may be gathered from a remark made by General Spaatz to General Arnold, that he hoped 'the AEAF plan (The Transportation Plan) will be repudiated by Tedder of his own accord, thus avoiding hard feelings.'

The real crux of the argument lay probably in the use of air power as an independent air weapon, and its use, as Ehrman put it, 'within the context of other operations.'

While the arguments and counter arguments were pursued hotly throughout March both plans were virtually in operation. 'Pointblank', designed as an operation in support of 'Overlord' had been in action for a full nine months. Tedder's 'Transportation Plan' had been partially in operation since the beginning of the year. Neither plan was, therefore, wholly speculative.

The original 'Transportation Plan' put forward in January by Allied

Expeditionary Air Force Headquarters was based on an analysis by Professor Zuckerman. It called for a sustained 90-day attack directed against 72 carefully chosen targets, 39 of them in Germany and 33 in France and Belgium. The plan, constantly shorn of its targets, which were subject to constant pressures and permutations from air, civil and military authorities, operated on a limited basis while the arguments were being hotly debated. The strategic views expressed by General Spaatz, Air Chief Marshal Harris and their supporters, were that it would be quixotic and totally wrong to divert strength from the main bomber offensive at a time when it was beginning to take powerful effect; and, secondly, that railways and marshalling yards were notoriously difficult targets, and that no effective slow-down of enemy transport would be achieved in time for 'D day'.

Assessments of early results by Air Intelligence, by SHAEF G-2, and by 21st Army Group Headquarters, pointed to almost total failure of the effort. As late as the 9th May, 21st Army Group, more directly concerned in the end results than any other body, referred to the 'Transportation Plan', as 'Pin-pricking on rail communications'. They were frankly scornful.

Never have assessments been more wide of the mark. The enemy communications were at the point of almost total collapse, for it was misleading simply to count trains and engines destroyed. Hundreds of engines, physically still 'in existence', were on the verge of breakdown, and the maintenance and repair facilities had sustained such a hammering, that it would prove impossible to get most of the battered trains on the move.

Nevertheless, at the height of his argument for the Transportation Plan most of the facts seemed to argue against Tedder. He stood as firm as a rock, convinced of the correctness of his view, and that nothing else would be of direct physical aid to 'Overlord'.

None of the difficulties had escaped Tedder. Even, he believed, if the enemy rail traffic could be reduced by 10 per cent by 'D day' it would be worth while. He and the Supreme Commander were convinced beyond a doubt that only in this way could air power make a direct contribution to 'Overlord'.

The arguments, heart-searchings, accompanied by constant changes of targets, and the inclusion of roads and bridges, continued almost up to the eve of 'D day', as also did the derogatory and derisory intelligence estimates of the effects on traffic, and of the 'load of hatred being generated in the hearts of the French people'. They were hopelessly wrong on both counts.

Throughout all the arguments and disagreements, covering command, strategy and tactics, the Allied Air Forces met all the great variety of demands upon them, and pursued their offensive with unabated vigour, while planning and training to lift three airborne divisions · simultaneously into Normandy. Even General Spaatz continued to hammer away at his oil targets, and one is inclined at times to wonder what all the fuss was about.

In March, a minor command crisis followed Leigh-Mallory's establishment of an advanced headquarters of AEAF under Air Marshal Sir Arthur Conyngham to operate in direct support of the ground forces. The objections of the bomber commanders to this appointment may not have been more than a last sop to their prejudices. In spite of everything Operation 'Pointblank' had operated for a full ten months by the eve of 'D day'. Up to the end of March, with the combined bomber offensive the aims were:

1) The reduction of the German Air Force.
2) The general reduction of the German war potential.
3) The weakening of the will of the German people.

In the last phases the direct demands of 'Overload', and of the assault landing, 'Neptune', took priority with five primary tasks.

1) To attain and to maintain an air situation whereby the German Air Force was rendered incapable of effective interference with Allied operations.
2) To provide continuous reconnaissance of enemy dispositions and movements.
3) To disrupt enemy communications

and supply channels for reinforcement.

4) To deliver offensive strikes against enemy naval forces.

5) To provide air lift for airborne forces.

In the assault phase the plan was designed:

1) To protect the cross-Channel movement of assault forces against enemy air attack, and to assist the naval forces to protect the assault against enemy naval attacks.

2) To prepare the way for assault by neutralising the beaches.

3) To protect the landing beaches and shipping concentrations.

4) To dislocate enemy communications and movement control during assault.

In addition to all these tasks a sustained attack was pressed against the flying bomb sites and rocket bases, thus to stave off the threat to the assembly areas, the massed shipping, and all the intricate preparations within the range of the new weapons.

To meet these commitments Air Chief Marshal Leigh-Mallory disposed some 5,677 aircraft of the US 9th Air Force and the 2nd Tactical Air Force of the Royal Air Force. Of these, 3,011 were medium, light, fighter and fighter-bombers, and the remainder transport aircraft, gliders, reconnaissance and Artillery Observation Aircraft.

Between the 9th February and 'D day' these forces, aided by the heavy bombers of Combined Bomber Offensive, attacked 80 rail and road targets with 21,949 aircraft dropping 76,200 tons of bombs. 51 targets were destroyed, 25 severely damaged, and slight damage was caused to the remaining 4. On the 6th March Bomber Command made the first heavy attack on Trappes, some twenty miles to the north of Paris, claiming 190 direct hits. The final effect revealed the inadequacy of the existing intelligence estimates, and went some way towards justifying the claims of the Air Marshals that they 'felt' and 'thought' they were achieving their various objects. By 'D day' railway traffic within 150 miles of the battlefield was at least 75 per cent unusable, and the whole railway system of North-West Europe had been dislocated. Air photography, or even visual observation on the ground, failed to reveal the condition of locomotives and rolling stock still 'in existence', but often held together 'by the last cotter pin'.

Early in May, the Tactical Air Forces opened an all-out assault on trains, railway and road bridges over the Seine below Paris. Heavy attacks were pressed on Mantes-Gassicourt, Liége, Ghent, Courtrai, Lille, Hasselt, Louvain, Boulogne, Orleans, Metz, Mulhouse, Rheims, Troyes and Charleroi. The pattern of the bombing might as easily have been designed to isolate the Pas de Calais as Normandy, and did not reveal the planned area of the Allied assault. Substantially attacks against road and railway bridges over the River Loire waited upon the day. In the event every bridge serving the battlefield was down.

Attacks on radar installations, wireless telegraphy and navigational stations paralysed enemy signals, and made air and sea reconnaissance virtually impossible. A total of 49 coastal batteries covering the sea approaches were also attacked with some success, while the long-sustained assaults on the German Aircraft Industry had reduced production by some 60 per cent. It was known that more than 5,000 enemy aircraft had been destroyed in combat between the middle of November and 'D day'. These facts combined with the constant harassing of airfields, and the enemy losses in trained pilots, effectively banished enemy air interference from the battlefield.

An important side-issue of the offensive against the railways was that 18,000 men of the 'Todt Organisation' were forced off urgent work on the strengthening of the 'Atlantic Wall' to undertake the more even urgent tasks of railway repair.

In the last weeks before 'D day' enemy troops, many of them of calibre, lay almost helpless under Allied bombs by night and day.

Such is a brief glimpse of the whelming contribution of air power in direct support of the Normandy landings. It was enough.

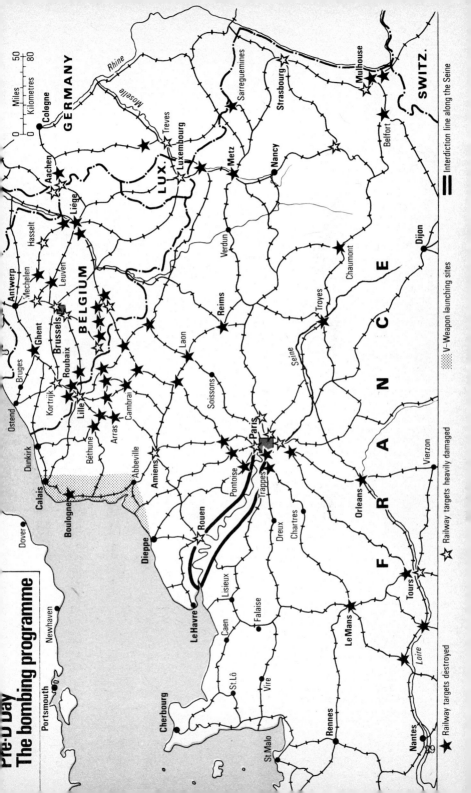

GERMANY

Cologne

Rhine

Moselle

Treves

Aachen

LUX.

Luxembourg

Liège

Hasselt

Antwerp

Mechelen

Leuven

BELGIUM

Ghent

Brussels

Bruges

Roubaix

Ostend

Kortrijk

Lille

Béthune

Dunkirk

Arras

Cambrai

Calais

Abbeville

Boulogne

Amiens

Dover

Dieppe

Rouen

Newhaven

Portsmouth

Pontoise

Trappes

Le Havre

Lisieux

Caen

Falaise

St.Lô

Vire

Cherbourg

St.Malo

Rennes

Nantes

Loire

Le Mans

Tours

Vierzon

Orleans

Chartres

Dreux

Paris

Soissons

Laon

Reims

Seine

Troyes

Chaumont

Dijon

FRANCE

Verdun

Metz

Nancy

Sarreguemines

Strasbourg

Belfort

Mulhouse

SWITZ.

Miles 50
Kilometres 80
0

Sarreguemines

Railway targets destroyed

Railway targets heavily damaged

V–Weapon launching sites

Interdiction line along the Seine

29

The Western Allies

The final presentation of the combined 'D day' plans took place under the supervision of SHAEF at a conference held at St Paul's School on the 15th May before a distinguished gathering, which included the British Monarch, the Prime Minister, Field Marshal Smuts, the most revered 'Elder Statesman' in the British Commonwealth, the Chiefs of Staff, the Supreme Commander, and his senior commanders of the three services.

The plan in its final shape belonged to General Sir Bernard Montgomery, the Ground Force Commander; Admiral Sir Bertram Ramsay, Commander-in-Chief Allied Naval Expeditionary Force; and Air Chief Marshal Sir Trafford Leigh-Mallory, Commander-in-Chief Allied Expeditionary Air Force. For five months the headquarters of these three had built upon the solid foundations laid by Cossac and his Allied staff. The final work bore many 'signatures', owing its existence to the constant planning of Naval and Combined Operations Headquarters, and the original 'Combined Commanders'.

By the 15th May, the plan had expanded west of the Vire estuary to the beaches of the Cotentin Pensinsula, and eastward to the Orne. Its three divisions in the assault lift had become five, supplemented by 14 tank regiments, commando and special service troops. The airborne lift had grown from two-thirds of a division, for which Cossac had not been granted sufficient air transport, to three airborne divisions. The naval tasks had expanded steadily in proportion Nevertheless, the plan remained fundamentally the creation of Cossac His was the miracle. He had been forced to build with shadows, spinning invisible webs, and sustained by drive and faith. Immediately upon the appointment of the Supreme Commander, and his indefatigable 'Ground Force Commander' the shadows had become real; the men and materials of war in immense quantity, for which Cossac had nagged and argued for months, lacking always the essential 'authority', swiftly filled the camps, the training grounds, the vast dumps, the harbours. Long before the 15th May, it would have been difficult to find a berth for a canoe round the British coasts. Invasion shipping overflowed into the Humber, Clyde and Belfast. Ships for convoys after 'D day' were held in Scottish ports. Shipping involved in the commerce without which the Island could not survive was routed to the Thames. Even an enemy able to observe from the air would have been unlikely to make head or tail of it. Dummy landing craft lay berthed in the commands of Dover and The Nore. Phoenix and Whale units, Bombardons and Beetles, and all the profuse and peculiar sections of the Mulberries lay off Selsey and Dungeness, sprouted from dry and wet docks and on the banks of the Thames, looking, at least to the eyes of Lieut-General Walter Bedell Smith,

Chief of Staff to the Supreme
Commander, like 'six-storey office
buildings lying on their sides.' Tugs,
as well as landing craft, remained in
desperately short supply.

The 'Q' appreciation, produced by
the Military Quartermaster-General's
Department, was a masterpiece of
administrative detail providing for
every demand of the commanders, not
only for 'D day', but far beyond.
Success would depend upon the
smooth and constant flow of men and
machines and ammunition. Much
would depend on the Mulberries .

The target date – 'Y day' – was the
1st June. The day 'D day' – would
follow at the earliest possible moment
thereafter. The earliest possible
moment was Y plus 4. The conditions
essential for the assault had been
agreed between the Supreme Commander and Admiral Sir Bertram
Ramsay on the 1st May. The extensive
mine-laying operations of the enemy,
coupled with the great mass of mined
obstacles sprouting from the beaches
and planted far out beyond the low
water mark, called for a landing on a
rising tide as soon after low tide as
possible, and in daylight as near to
dawn as possible. A moon was desir-
able by night. These considerations
fixed the possible dates as the 5th, 6th
and 7th June. The 5th and 6th were
both good, the 7th not so good. After
that, no further opportunity would
occur until the 19th June, and without
the moon.

The possibility of a forced delay of

two weeks, dire in its inferences, had
been planned for in all its stark detail.
It involved the halting of an avalanche
of men and supplies, and all that must
go with them, already on shipboard,
and half of them at sea. A million
more men, armour, artillery, transport, and a million tons of supplies
were in the pipe-lines, converging on
the embarkation points; a million
more behind them, reaching back
across the Atlantic.

The thought made men shudder.
'The problems arising out of a postponement of 12–14 days to the next
suitable period are too appalling even
to contemplate,' wrote Admiral
Ramsay. Nevertheless, the problems
were fully contemplated, and the
implications faced.

On the 8th May, the Supreme Commander tentatively agreed 'D day'
with his commanders on land, sea and
air, as the 5th June. The Navy and Air
Force had been laying mines for three
weeks to protect the convoys; the far
more complex task of mine-sweeping
lay ahead. Ten channels to Normandy
must be swept from the assembly
point known to the Royal Navy as
'Piccadilly Circus', and officially as
'Area Z' just south of the Isle of Wight.
The state of the tide for the landing
meant that the mine-sweeping would
have to be done across the tide setting
strongly to the east in the opening
stages, and setting westward at about
the half-way mark. Mine-sweeping
had never before been carried out in
such conditions, and great difficulties

**Lieutenant General H. D. G. Crerar,
Canadian First Army**

in timing were involved. Twelve Mine-sweeping Flotillas were assembled for the job.

While the commanders issued their orders, and bore the great weight of responsibility, tens of thousands of men from petty officers and sergeants upwards worked out the detail of their fragments of the vast puzzle, co-ordinated and fitted together through a maze of commands into the final picture.

The return to the Continent, con-

**Lieutenant General M. C. Dempsey,
British 2nd Army**

ceived almost on the beaches of Dunkirk, and quickening under Cossac, had its final impetus from General Montgomery. He expressed himself in simple, uncompromising terms:

'The assault was an operation requiring a single co-ordinated plan of action under one commander; I therefore became Overall Land-Force Commander responsible to the Supreme Commander for planning and executing the military aspect of the assault, and subsequent capture of the lodgement area.'

On the 1st February, Montgomery, Ramsay and Leigh-Mallory produced the 'Neptune' Initial Joint Plan, 'an executive instrument' covering the expansion of 'Overlord'. The Air Forces were already embarked upon the preliminary stages of the battle. The Navy had begun administrative planning in May 1942, and the whole framework of its immense carrying, offensive and defensive task was already in detail. It would continue to expand and adapt until 'D day' and far beyond 'D day'. The armies to be involved faced a gigantic ordeal of planning. Under 21st Army Group Headquarters the US 1st Army and the British 2nd Army produced their outline assault plans on the 25th February and the 20th March respectively. From that moment detailed planning went ahead on all levels, the military 'Q' Staffs bearing the greater part of the burden.

By the end of the first week of April, Montgomery, with the Commanders of the Naval and Air Forces, was able to announce his full plans to his General Officers, and hammer out the possibilities with his Senior Field Officers. His intention, as he expressed it, was:

'To assault, simultaneously, beaches on the Normandy coast immediately north of the Carentan Estuary and between the Carentan Estuary and the River Orne, with the object of securing as a base for further operations a lodgement area.'

The lodgement area must include, at the earliest possible moment, airfield sites south-eastward of the important road centre of Caen, and the port of Cherbourg. He expounded his plan to develop a major threat to break out on the eastern flank, thus to draw the main weight of the enemy reserves and strength against the British and Canadians. Having established a firm hinge pivoting upon Caen, and drawn the enemy to full commitment in the east he would break out with Bradley's US armies to cut a wide swathe 'to cut off all the enemy forces south of the Seine, over which river the bridges were to be destroyed by air action.'

The US 1st Army, with three Regimental Combat Teams, would assault astride the Carentan Estuary, to capture Cherbourg and develop their attack southward upon St. Lô to conform to the British 2nd Army.

The British 2nd Army, with five brigades, would assault between Asnelles and Ouistreham, with the Canadians in the centre, to develop a bridgehead south of a line St. Lô, Caen, and south-east of Caen to secure airfield sites and to protect the eastern flank of the US 1st Army.

Both armies would be supported by specialised engineer troops, armour, commandos and US Rangers.

The US 82nd and 101st Airborne Divisions would land south-east and west of St Mère Eglise, astride the flooded Merderet river, to capture crossings and to secure the line of the Douve river, thereby to assist the seaborne assault on 'Utah' beach and prevent the movement of enemy reserves into the Cotentin.

The British 6th Airborne Division would land east of Caen to seize

Lieutenant General Carl Spaatz, Commander U.S. Strategic Air Forces

crossings over the Orne river at Bénouville and Ranville.

It was hoped to land 1,500 tanks, 5,000 tracked fighting vehicles, 3,000 guns and 10,500 vehicles ranging from jeeps to bulldozers on 'D day'. Such in broad outline was the land force task.

The US forces were on the right, the western flank, for reasons of supply. As soon as Cherbourg and the Brittany ports could be opened they would be supplied direct from the

General H. H. Arnold, Commanding U.S. Army Air Forces, with Lt-Gen Omar H. Bradley

United States. The British would finally rely upon the Channel ports and Antwerp. In the meantime all would rely upon the two Mulberries and the five Gooseberries .

The enemy were expected to hold some sixty divisions in the West under Field Marshal von Rundstedt. Montgomery's immediate opponent would be Field Marshal Rommel, commanding Army Group B, consisting of the German 7th Army in Normandy and Brittany, the 15th Army in the Pas de Calais and Flanders, and the 88th Corps in Holland. The greatest concentration of enemy strength behind the most powerful fortifications lay in the Pas de Calais. It had been the business of the Allies throughout many months, by feints, rumours, diversions, to keep them there, and to bolster the natural enemy fears based on the simple proposition that a straight line is the shortest distance between two points.

But since his appointment, Field Marshal Rommel had striven with all his energies to reinforce the defences of the Bay of Seine. The heavy batteries of Cherbourg and Le Havre, supported by at least thirty others, overlapped the whole area, and could drench the sea approaches and the beaches with fire. Behind the great mass of obstacles and mines planted in the sea approaches and the beaches lay anti-tank defences, concrete strong points and earth works backed by a formidable countryside ideally suited to defence. The natural water system and marshland behind the Carentan Estuary had lent itself to inundations confining the beach exits to narrow causeways, impassable to men without armour. These inundations were particularly extensive in the Varreville sector, code-named 'Utah', and behind the first water barriers a belt of floods followed the courses of the Merderet and Douve rivers west and south from Carentan.

The British and Canadians also had their special problems in their difficult approaches, in the maze of small villages linked together in a system of strong points immediately behind the coasts, and beyond them the 'Bocage', a patchwork of small fields, tall hedgerows, steep banks and ditches, and deep narrow lane cuttings, a countryside of death traps forty miles deep, hopeless for armour. South-east of Caen lay the open plain, but that was a long way from 'D day'.

Air Chief Marshal Sir Trafford Leigh-Mallory explained the main tasks of the British 2nd and the U S 9th Tactical Air Forces in close support. On the 'Day' the air forces would maintain a sustained density of ten fighter squadrons over the beaches, five British and five American. Six squadrons would be alerted to support the beach cover. Five squadrons would cover the main Naval approaches, and a striking force of 33 fighter squadrons would be in reserve.

Following the fulfilment of escort duties for the Airborne troops a total of 171 squadrons would be apportioned, 54 squadrons to beach cover, 15 squadrons to shipping cover, 36 squadrons to direct support, 33 squadrons to offensive operations and bomber escort, and 33 squadrons as a striking force.

Admiral Sir Bertram Ramsay expressed himself with great simplicity in defining the Naval rôle. The initial success must depend upon the Naval Forces. His Operational Orders of the 10th April read:

'The object of the Naval C. in C. is the timely arrival of the assault forces at their beaches, the cover of their landings, and subsequently the support and maintenance and the rapid build-up of our forces ashore.'

In round figures, some 5,000 ships and 4,000 ship-to-shore craft, would be at the service of the assault. Their fire power, from the heavy armament of the battleships and cruisers down to the destroyers, the rocket ships, the armour and artillery firing from their craft on the run-in, was truly colossal

Operation 'Neptune' would launch Operation 'Overlord'.

Meanwhile, the Russians, pressing the Germans hard through all February, March and April had crossed the Dnieper and the Bug, and on the 8th April, while Montgomery was in the midst of his Staff discussions on the 'D day' plans at St. Paul's School Tolbukhin opened his assault on the Perekop defences, and began the brilliant reconquest of the Crimea. At the same time the Russians were informed of the Allied plans and the target date of 'D day'. They would synchronise their own great summer offensive with the Western Allies. By the middle of May the great battle in Italy was also moving to its conclusion.

The problems confronting General Eisenhower were on an infinitely wider stage than those with which either his Deputy, Air Chief Marshal Tedder, or his 'Ground Force Commander', General Montgomery, had to deal, or to consider. As the representative and voice of the US Joint Chiefs of Staff in Britain he was in constant consultation with the British Chiefs of Staff and the Prime Minister on matters of deep political significance and major strategy. Furthermore, it was his duty to act upon the directives of his Chiefs in Washington, to advance and argue their views even when they differed from his own opinions. Fearful of being unduly influenced by the eloquence of the British Prime Minister on the one hand, and the concise strategical reasonings of the CIGS on the other, his physical presence in the country and his consequent nearness to many home problems often engaged his sympathies and understanding much more closely than those of Washington.

A random selection of difficult issues might include the Allied attitude to General de Gaulle and the future of France, the problems of civil and military affairs in liberated countries, psychological warfare, the dismemberment of Nazi Germany, a subject upon which the United States, Soviet Russia and Britain, shared a basic agreement, the implications of 'Unconditional Surrender', and the relative merits of Berlin and the Ruhr as military objectives. On the fringes of his spheres of direct interest were such matters as the Soviet absorption of the Baltic States, their boundaries with Poland, and the inclusion of Bessarabia within their territory.

Decisions to restrict civilian movement, degrees of censorship, and kindred questions were carried out largely in accordance with his desires. He developed a genuine awareness of the sacrifices of the British people, and disliked asking for more. When space had to be found to berth and unload forty ships from the United States filled with munitions of war, and it could only be done at a direct cost of 500,000 tons of civilian supplies of food, he appealed to the President of the United States to do something about it. It was a direct case of 'guns before butter'. Deprived of coastwise shipping in the cause of the cross-Channel attack, the railways loaded to the last gramme with materials of war, this seemed almost a 'last straw.'

The Supreme Commander had undergone an astounding metamorphosis from obscurity to a position of immense power and authority, involving innumerable questions which were not only outside the range of his knowledge, but opposed to the principles of his West Point training. It is not surprising that by the middle of May he had begun to show signs of strain. He was saved by his natural simplicity, and his remarkable innocence. It is doubtful whether a handful of men existed in the world with the gifts or 'qualifications' for such a task: it must be equally doubtful whether any gifts or qualifications could have served the Supreme Commander, or the Alliance, better, or as well, as those he possessed.

From the moment of his arrival in Britain, Eisenhower had set about the task of establishing a closely knit team, insisting with firmness upon

Major General Percy C S Hobart

Above: Churchill Mk III AVRE 'Bobbin'

Below: Churchill Mk VIII 'Crocodile'

DDs, Crabs, and AVREs were designed to get ashore and neutralise the defences – but they would never be able to get near those defences if the beach surface should prove unable to bear their weight. Hence the Bobbin, another AVRE fitting, which could lay down a canvas mat approximately 110 yards long, passed beneath the tank.
Armament: one Petard spigot mortar, one ·303-inch machine-gun. Crew: four. Speed while laying mat: 3 mph. Range: 87 miles. Weight: 39 tons

The Crocodile was at once the most horrific and spectacular of the 'Funnies': a flamethrowing tank, which carried 400 gallons of flame-gun fuel in its trailer. Compressed nitrogen forced the fuel from trailer to flame-gun (mounted in the normal machine-gun position), giving a range of about 120 yards.
Armament: one 75-mm gun. Crew: five. Speed: 12 mph. Range: 125 miles. Weight: 40 tons

Above: Sherman M4-A4 'Firefly'

The Firefly was the first successful
Allied attempt to match the gun-power
of the German tanks. This was essential,
for the German Panther and Tiger tanks
were already known to be formidable –
and the result was the Firefly, which
mounted the British 17-pounder heavy
anti-tank gun on the hull of the well-tried
Sherman tank.
*Armament: one 17-pounder gun, one
50-inch machine-gun. Crew: five.
Speed: 25mph. Range: 120 miles.
Weight: 32·9 tons*

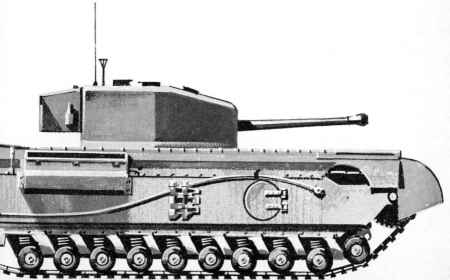

Right: Sherman M4-A4 DD (Duplex Drive)

The DD tanks would be the first weapons to reach the shore. A DD was a swimming tank, powered by the tank's engines, and kept afloat by a collapsible canvas screen which was lowered on landing, thus permitting the tank's guns to be immediately brought to bear on the enemy defences.
Armament: one 75-mm gun, two 300-inch machine-guns, one 50-inch machine-gun. Crew: five. Speed: 4½ knots afloat, 25 mph on land. Land range: 120 miles. Weight: 33 tons

Below: Churchill Mk III AVRE (SBG)

Enemy anti-tank walls and ditches were to be tackled by AVREs which were adapted to carry either huge brushwood fascines, or SBG – the Small Box Girder bridge, dropped over the obstacle by firing a small shearing charge above the turret.
Armament: one Petard spigot mortar, one 303-inch machine-gun. Crew: four. Speed: 16 mph. Range: 87 miles. Weight (tank only) 39 tons

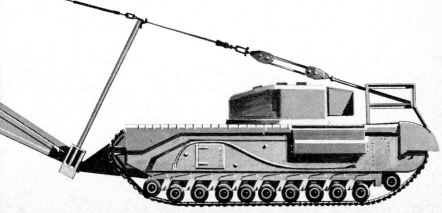

Above: Churchill Mk III AVRE

The AVRE – Armoured Vehicle Royal Engineers – was specially designed to concentrate on knocking out pillboxes and blockhouses at short range with its 'flying dustbin' heavy mortar bombs. *Armament: one 25-pounder Petard spigot mortar, one ·303-inch machine-gun. Crew: five. Speed: 16 mph. Range: 87 miles. Weight: 39 tons*

Below: Sherman M4-A4 'Crab' Flail

The Crab was a minesweeping tank: on landing, its task was to advance into the beach minefield defences, flailing a lane 10 feet wide through which the main landing forces could pour. *Armament: one 75-mm gun, two ·300-inch machine-guns, one ·50-inch machine-gun. Crew: five. Sweeping speed: $1\frac{1}{2}$ mph. Weight: 33 tons*

absolute co-operation, and the sinking of 'National prejudices'. He succeeded admirably except on a high level. In his first address to the Officers of his Staff at Norfolk House he said:

'We are not allies. We have plenty of allies among the United Nations, but we who are to undertake this great operation are one indivisible force with all its points more closely integrated than has ever been the case before.''

The prides and prejudices of two vastly different peoples, the differences of their military, political and social outlooks and behaviour, engendered by their history, their geography, their origins, and all these the more apparent because of the misleading similarities of language, were overcome to a remarkable degree by the tact and determination of the Supreme Commander.

In the upshot Eisenhower was well served. His Chief of Staff, Lieut - General Walter Bedell Smith would have been outstanding in any army for the quality of his thinking, and the virtues of his pessimism. He regarded the establishment of a 'lodgement' in France as a 'fifty-fifty' chance. On the factors known to the Allies, and the unknown factors, such as the success or otherwise of the Mulberries , it was a brave estimate. As Deputy Chief of Staff, the British Lieut.-General Morgan had an unriva. ed knowledge of the intricacies of 'Overlord'. Tedder gave the Supreme Commander freedom from the awkward burden of Command of the Air Forces. Lieut - General Sir Humphrey Gale was his principal adviser on logistics, and the British Major-General Whiteley was a member of the tactical and operational team. Few men have been better served than the Supreme Commander, and that he was so served is a tribute to his particular 'genius'.

British troops liked him for reasons completely the reverse of those which endeared Montgomery to them. In scores of letters 'home' British soldiers commented upon the Supreme Commander's simple and unadorned uniform, his lack of medal ribbons and 'brass', his quiet manner, friendliness and confidence, and his air of command. Eisenhower was something entirely new in 'top brass' to them, but he was 'Top Brass alright.'

These reactions, and many more, were being carefully noted by hundreds of Allied Censor Officers imprisoned in bleak rooms, and wading through tens of thousands of letters each day, making digests of current thinking, and morale. All mail, telephone calls and cables to the United States had been stopped, and for a month there would be a vacuum of news – which in itself was 'news' – in tens of thousands of homes. The pile-up of troops mail was colossal. Security demanded these minimum precautions, but the security risk on the overwhelming majority of letters was negligible.

In all their rounds of visiting troops the most important visits made by the Supreme Commander and his principal commanders on land, were to the training grounds of Hobart's armour. The 79th Armoured Division had grown to proportions far exceeding a normal armoured division. Its assault squadrons, fully trained in the management of their strange and ingenious collection of fighting vehicles were organised to be placed at the service of British and Canadian units and formations. In the last weeks, faced with a new beach problem, 'Bobbins' had been devised from which carpets of coir and tubular scaffolding could be laid to enable the armour to walk over sands and dunes.

Eisenhower, Montgomery and Bradley watched demonstrations of all that the armour could achieve in opening the 'Atlantic Wall'. Conditions of the utmost realism had been created. Eisenhower was greatly impressed, and said that he would like to make use of everything. Bradley seemed to show interest, but did not commit himself. Montgomery, however, believed that the 79th Armoured was a winner. He went into detail exhaustively, and following careful analysis and demonstration, made his choices. The flails, mine-sweeping Sherman tanks, would lead the van of the British and Canadian assaults, supported by flamethrowers, and DD swimming tanks. Engineers in armour would lead the way. Bradley decided to avail himself only of DD tanks. These decisions were of great significance.

General Bradley's visits to his

troops were in a different key to those of the Supreme Commander and of General Montgomery. He was at great pains to make his visits informal, to see his men 'as they were', and he even went to the lengths of sacking a battalion commander who had 'put on a show' for his benefit. Quietly, methodically, he tramped South-West England, calling on small groups of men, trying to discover their temper. Bradley was always a man who would squat down on his haunches, chew a blade of grass and talk as an equal to any man.

There were in May, eleven American Divisions in Britain, only one of which had been under fire. This was the US 1st Division, which had seen service in the Mediterranean, and resented Bradley's inevitable decision to give it the spearhead rôle in the assault upon 'Omaha' beach. The US 29th Division, the first comers to Britain, while claiming first rights to lead, had developed morbid fears of casualties. Without doubt General Bradley bore a heavy burden, and bore it squarely. His troops were 'green', but well trained. Naturally they lacked the basic feeling about the war and the coming assault of their British counterparts. They had not been driven out of France, bombed and machine-gunned on the beaches, hemmed into their homeland under threat of invasion and under fire from the air, and on short rations for four long years. The struggle against the Germans throughout the Twentieth Century was not something they had absorbed with their mother's milk. They were, in fact, a long way from home, in a foreign land, and about to assault another foreign land. It promised to be highly dangerous. They did not feel that they were liberating either themselves or anybody else. All this was natural.

The psychological approach of the US Command to their troops would have had a distressing effect on British morale. They were lectured on the 'miracles of modern combat medicine', advanced methods of dealing with casualties, and inspired by articles in their Army newspaper. Those evincing particular dread of 'the shock and pain of battle' were talked to candidly by their commanders. Newspaper articles stressed the vicious policies and beliefs of the enemy, and the necessity of dealing ruthlessly with him, while Eisenhower charged his Commanders 'to overcome any lack of will to fight on the part of their troops by explaining the critical importance of defeating the Germans.'

On the military level the careful briefings of the troops were methodical, realistic and of obvious value. Accurate models of the sections of beach gave men a visual knowledge of their own rôles. At the same time the last activities which must mean assault imminent even to the least suspicious were in full swing in the last week of May. In that last burst of glorious weather tens of thousands of vehicles were waterproofed, invasion money and sea-sick pills were issued, weapons checked. By the end of May men and machines were loading into their ships, and from the most distant ports of Britain some of the vital parts of 'Neptune' set their courses for the South, to the rendezvous.

At a quarter-past-ten on the night of Friday, 2nd June, two midget submarines, X20 and X23, under command of Lieut Honour, cleared the East Gate of the Portsmouth boom and joined their escorting trawlers for the voyage to France. In the early morning light of Saturday they dived offshore to watch and wait unseen but seeing the enemy. The weather had deteriorated horribly. It was the one vital factor out of the hands of men.

It was difficult, in the last days, for any man or woman in Britain involved in the humblest degree in the vast effort of 'D day', to imagine that anything else existed. The thing itself seemed 'total'. But to appreciate the Allied cross-Channel assault it is important to glance at it in the perspective of the framework of 'total war'. The United States was not yet at the peak of her war effort, her heavy commitment in the Pacific was moving steadily towards its climax in growing strength. Assault plans for the invasion of Japan, which would dwarf even 'Overlord', were already far advanced, involving the Chiefs of Staff and the heads of Government in the United States and Britain in complex discussions.

In Italy an American army fought

under Alexander with British, Canadians and Free French, and was preparing for the final heave which would encompass the rout of Kesselring.

Going out from the United States, with its enormous reserves of wealth, its massive productive capacity, and its manpower, this effort, great as it was, helps to reveal something of the nature of Britain's war effort as she embarked on the last phase of the desperate struggle against time. For four years she had been at full stretch, fighting in theatres of war embracing the Atlantic, the Arctic and Indian Oceans, the Mediterranean and many lesser seas. Her armies had toiled and fought through North Africa and large parts of the Middle East, achieving victories little short of miraculous under Wavell and Auchinleck, and at last the reward of Alamein under Montgomery, but in the dark months between suffering agonies of defeat and frustration on the fringes of many lands. Her troops had fought up through Sicily and Italy, and were crawling through the steaming jungles of South-East Asia. Now, impoverished, her manpower dwindling fast, compelled perhaps to barter her autonomy, she knew only that victory in 1944 might save her. Steadily the 'terms of war' had moved against her, placing her more at the mercy of her friends than of her enemies, and she had come doggedly, even bravely, to the eve of her 'last throw'.

But the present left little time for thought of the future. In the midst of the final preparations for the assault on North-West Europe the Combined Chiefs of Staff and the heads of government wrestled with a host of problems. General de Gaulle, indignant at the denial of recognition to his provisional government, refused at the last to permit French Liaison Officers to embark with the Allies for France. Of a different order were the discussions on Pacific strategy, which involved India and Australia. Throughout the month of May the Conference of the Dominion Prime Ministers met in London.

Random selections from the diary of war reveal some of the dark shadows of the fears consuming the Prime Minister. On the 12th April, hoping even then to stave off the South of France landings, he emphasised to President Roosevelt the great contribution to 'Overlord' of the Italian campaign. It had drawn, held, and was defeating thirty-five German divisions of quality. How could we have hoped for more, or expected so much! Surely a series of 'feints' would suffice to hold the few German divisions in the South of France! How, in any case, could such a landing effect the battle for Normandy?

It had all been said before. The United States was no longer prepared even to argue. She would have her way, not only in the South of France, but in Italy, even in Britain and Western Europe. Not for nothing had she agreed to put 'Germany first'.

On the 29th April, the threat of famine in Bengal compelled the diversion of urgently needed shipping from Australia to carry grain to avert a disaster which, in its death roll, would dwarf the casualties of war. Mountbatten was forced again to improvise in South East Asia with his accustomed skill and ingenuity. Soon his armies would be forgotten.

Yet in May 1944, Britain as a nation was still a long way from despair. Outwardly there was cause for rejoicing. The final offensive in Italy opened on the 11th May, and on the 18th Cassino fell. Five days later the Anzio beachhead at last linked in with the main offensive, and while the British Eighth Army pursued the enemy up the Tiber valley, intent upon its encirclement and destruction, the Americans raced for the symbol of Rome, entering the Piazza Venezia thirty-five hours before the Allied forces landed on the Normandy beaches.

'The cop is the thing that matters', Churchill cabled to Alexander, but the 'cop' was Rome. The great Russian Summer Offensive was then only ten days away, and as the Allied power closed in upon the Germans from three sides, the 'Ghost of Anvil' on the Southern horizon haunted Alexander, and nagged at Churchill in London.

The voice of Britain was no longer heard.

The enemy

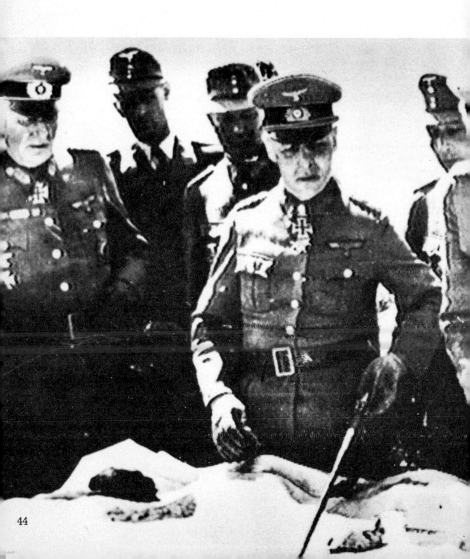

The Nazi power reached and passed its military climacteric in the summer of 1942. By the autumn her fortunes were in marked decline.

All that was in the balance was not the final collapse in utter ruin of Nazi Germany, but the nature and timing of the collapse. There were Germans, professional soldiers such as von Brauchitsch and General Beck, even perhaps von Rundstedt and Halder, idealists such as von Stauffenberg, pastors such as Niemöller, who saw these things from the beginning, or quickly discovered them, but at the summit there towered a maniac perverting the German mind and spirit.

With her military power in decline,

Hitler's unchallenged power was manifest. Col -General Franz Halder stated to his interrogators that there were, no long-range planning studies after October, 1942, 'because these would only have reached conclusions which Hitler would not accept'. Progressively from October 1942, Hitler sacrificed the German armies, and no man could stop him.

Whereas the Grand Strategy of the Western Allies was blurred by the conflicting interests of the three main Allies, the Grand Strategy of the enemy did not exist. He merely reacted. In Africa, Rommel, never adequately supported, was deprived of the genuine chances of victory in Egypt, then abandoned and forced to sacrifice the Afrika Korps in Tunisia. From north to south over the vast Eastern Front whole armies were consumed by the Russians. Von Paulus with more than 250,000 men was condemned to unnecessary destruction at Stalingrad. But it was the failure of Field Marshal List in his attempted drive through the Caucasus that marked the change in Hitler. In a long statement to Capt B. H. Liddell Hart, General Walter Warlimont explained Hitler's reaction when Jodl, returning from the Caucasus, confronted him with mistakes he could not, even in the dim recesses of his distorted mind, put upon anyone else. His whole manner and behaviour changed from that moment. He seldom left his hut. He ate alone. 'I am convinced', stated Warlimont, ' that Hitler, when confronted with the actual situation at the end of the second offensive against Russia, suddenly grasped that he would never reach his goal in the East, and that the war would be eventually lost'.[1]

The judgement does not rest on the word of Warlimont. It is confirmed by Jodl and many others, above all by the facts of history. Throughout 1943, the Armies of Nazi Germany suffered appalling losses, inevitably, because they were the raw material of the tragedy in which they were caught up. Since there could not be victory, there must be defeat. No other end was possible. The numbers of divisions remained; their quality and content deteriorated at an ever - increasing pace.

Meanwhile, the year 1943 had brought complete victory for the Allies in the Atlantic, cleared the Mediterranean, and begun the relentless destruction of German Industry, and the steady reduction of the German Air force. On the Eastern front the sombre sacrifice of the German Armies continued to the point when only despair might fill the vacuum of the German soul.

From the moment of the Nazi offensive against Russia her forces had been totally inadequate for the defence of the 3,000 miles of Western coastline she controlled. Field Marshal von Rundstedt, transferred from his Command in the West in April 1941, to command the Southern Group of Armies for the attack against Russia, confessed that the bareness at his back gave him a feeling of chill. He expected Britain to walk in. This is not only illustrative of the Nazi weakness in the West, but of the enemy ignorance of the true condition of the almost unarmed remnants of the British Army that had survived Dunkirk. Such thinking helped to save Britain from invasion.

Returning to command in the West in 1942, von Rundstedt found the situation little more to his liking. Throughout that year France had been used as a rest area for divisions badly mauled on the Eastern Front. The 50 or 60 divisions available at all material times on paper seldom mustered 25 field divisions of reasonable quality, and seldom at full strength. A Nazi decision that it would be more profitable to use prisoners of war as soldiers rather than to exterminate them, or induce them to rot in their 'Belsens' led to a complex situation, but it relieved the growing strain on German manpower. In 1942, foreign battalions were being drafted into German divisions, and Major Milton Shulman noted that in one German Regiment no fewer than eight different kinds of 'Pay Book' were in use, covering at least a score of Eastern 'tribes'. A hotch-potch of races under German officers made up at least 10 per cent of the strength of many divisions, and up to 25 per cent of the strength of a few.

It can be seen at a glance, and it was seen at a glance by von Rundstedt, that 50 or 60 divisions, even of the highest quality, will 'go' at least ten times too many into 3,000 miles of coastline. One division to three miles was not excessive in defence; one division in 50 or 60 miles was hopeless. One of the main enemy problems, therefore, was to decide where as well as when a major assault from the West might be expected. Whatever decision was made, wide areas must be left bare. The problem of reserves became insoluble.

The appreciation of Field Marshal von Rundstedt, which remained constant, was that the Western Allies would assault against the Pas de Calais area, probably astride the Somme, not only because it was the shortest route from shore to shore, simplifying sea and air cover and a quick turn-round, but because it offered the shortest route to the Rhine, and on into the heart of the Reich. The fact that it was obvious could not exclude it and the view from France was very different from the view from Britain. While the Allies saw the strength of the enemy positions von Rundstedt was acutely aware of the weaknesses. If the 'Atlantic Wall' was more than the 'propaganda structure' von Rundstedt considered it, it was also much less than Hitler had led himself or the Allies to imagine. The materials and labour were never available to carry out his dreams, and even had the dreams been practical the fate of the immensely powerful Maginot Line had proved that defences were no stronger than their weakest links, or their defenders. The 'Atlantic Wall' existed in something like its 'propaganda strength' in the Pas de Calais, and nowhere else.

Throughout 1943, as the Nazi armies were bled white in the East, and the Allied strategic bombing offensive moved steadily towards its terrible crescendo, von Rundstedt strove to reorganise the meagre and poor quality troops at his disposal. Static coastal divisions were formed, carrying a high proportion of second grade troops, but with the virtue of gaining familiarity with their allotted areas.

The Tension mounts. *Top right:* Rommel inspects his defences. *Bottom right:* the men who waited

The Allied landings in North Africa in the late Autumn of 1942 put Hitler 'constantly on the jump', in the words of General Blumentritt. He expected landings anywhere and everywhere. His anxieties included Holland, Portugal, Spain and the Adriatic. The fall of Tunis led him to believe that the South of France was immediately threatened. At the same time his fears for the vulnerability of Norway matched Churchill's recurrent desire to make these fears come true. It was an impossible situation for his Generals, almost all of whom were kept in ignorance of the progress of war outside their immediate command areas. In April, 1943, General von Schweppenburg, then commanding the 86th Corps, was ordered to prepare 'Operation Gisela' in which five mechanised divisions would fan-out through Spain, four divisions making a 'dash' for Madrid while the fifth anchored on Bilbao. It is not to be wondered at that he should describe the project as 'This folly'.

But although the Generals did not share the wide range of their Führer's haunting apprehensions they were compelled to act upon his hunches, especially when they pointed to the region of the Somme and Normandy.

In September 1943, the elaborate exercise carried out in Britain, partly as a rehearsal of the massive and complex troop movements and loading problems for 'Overlord', and partly to mislead the enemy, failed in its second purpose. The bluff, von Rundstedt thought, was 'too obvious', and it seems that the Germans were misled and alarmed more by the natural rumours abounding in the Occupied countries than by the stories planted by the Allies.

The Autumn of 1943, bringing with it the first heavy seas and the promise of winter, limited the areas of possible Allied attack, and brought a respite

**The Men who went. *Top left:* Last steps on the friendly shore.
Top right: British airborne troops black-up for the night drop.
Middle right: Some of the air armada which would drop them. *Bottom:* Old-fashioned but swift and silent. British commandos used bicycles to race like phantoms to target areas.**

to the enemy. All was probably secure until the Spring of 1944. All that could be done was to strengthen the 'Atlantic Wall', increase the minefields guarding the approaches, and improve the training and rather miscellaneous weapon strength of the available troops. The placing and use of the armoured reserve was already looming as a difficult matter, and one which the suspicions of Hitler combined with the Air power of the allies would make impossible.

Through the year the quality of the French Resistance had greatly improved, the quarrels of the various groups had abated, and the whole movement had responded well to British aid and organisation. By the winter of 1943–44 the Resistance had become a serious problem for the enemy, sabotaging railways and transport, and undermining morale with the fears that there might always be a bomb under the bed or in the wardrobe, that trains might leave the rails, or mysteriously blow up. And these things happened with growing frequency. The signs that the moment of crisis in the West was approaching could not be misread. 1944 would be the year, Western Europe the place, the spring or summer would bring the hour.

Information reaching the enemy through a German Foreign Office report dated 8th January, 1944, by way of Ankara, gave the code name of 'Overlock' to the Allied plans, and provided 'conclusive evidence that the Anglo-Saxons are determined to force a show-down by opening a "Second Front" in 1944. However, this Second Front will not be in the Balkans'.

An Intelligence analysis by the Chief of Western Military Intelligence followed a month later:

'For 1944 an operation is planned *outside the Mediterranean* that will seek to force a decision and, therefore, will be carried out with all available forces. This operation is probably being prepared under the code name of OVERLORD. The intention of committing large forces becomes clear from the fact that the operation is expected to produce the final military decision within a comparatively short period of time'.

The Atlantic Wall. *Top left:* As early as 1942, French civilians had been drafted to dig foundations. *Top right:* Early pill-box under camouflage. *Above:* The Teeth of the Defence; heavy artillery under bomb-proof canopy. *Left:* Rommel, the man responsible

Above right: Rommel inspecting Indian troops of the 'Free India' Army.
Right: Coastal artillery observation post. *Below:* Monument to the Chief Engineer

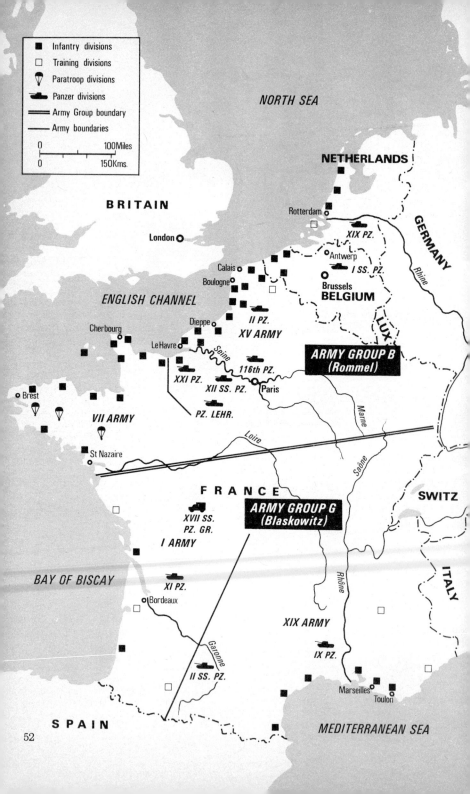

Legend:
- Infantry divisions
- Training divisions
- Paratroop divisions
- Panzer divisions
- Army Group boundary
- Army boundaries

0   100 Miles
0   150 Kms.

NORTH SEA

NETHERLANDS

Rotterdam

XIX PZ.

Antwerp

I SS. PZ.

Calais

Boulogne

Brussels
BELGIUM

BRITAIN

London

ENGLISH CHANNEL

Dieppe

II PZ.

XV ARMY

Cherbourg

Le Havre

Seine

116th PZ.

ARMY GROUP B
(Rommel)

GERMANY

Rhine

LUX

XXI PZ.

XII SS. PZ.

Paris

PZ. LEHR.

Brest

VII ARMY

Marne

St Nazaire

Loire

Saône

FRANCE

XVII SS.
PZ. GR.

ARMY GROUP G
(Blaskowitz)

SWITZ

I ARMY

BAY OF BISCAY

XI PZ.

Rhône

ITALY

Bordeaux

XIX ARMY

Garonne

IX PZ.

II SS. PZ.

Marseilles

Toulon

SPAIN

MEDITERRANEAN SEA

52

Above: Laying mines in the approach
roads. *Below:* The sea beyond . . .

The exact area to be attacked
eluded the enemy, but an Intelligence
report dated 21st February re-affirmed
that:

'The frequently expressed determination *to bring the war to an end in
1944 is to be considered the keynote of
the enemy's operational planning.* It is
also repeatedly mentioned as a definite
fact that the decision will be sought
by a *large scale attack in Western
Europe'.*

The enemy expected the attack
either in the first or the third quarter
of the year. His Balkan fears were at
an end. Time had narrowed down to
May–August, 1944; place could be
narrowed perhaps to the Pas de
Calais – or Normandy.

The appointment of Field Marshal
Rommel in November 1943, to inspect
and improve the defences of the
Western coastline from Denmark to
the Spanish Border, complicated an
already difficult command situation.
Possibly General Blumentritt exaggerated when he told Capt Liddell

Field-Marshal Erwin Rommel commanding Army Group B, with Field-Marshal von Rundstedt, C-in-C, West

Hart that, 'soon the armies did not know whether they were under command of Rundstedt or Rommel'. Rommel's direct line through to Hitler certainly invested him with great influence, but equally there is no doubt that he respected von Rundstedt, C in C West, and observed the proper etiquette. Von Rundstedt, while holding a poor opinion of Rommel as a strategist, has paid tributes to his courage and loyalty. In the hands of one of the Nazi upstarts the appointment would have rendered the position of the C in C intolerable.

It was, inevitably, an uneasy situation, eased over the months by Rommel's appointment to command Army Group B, with responsibility under von Rundstedt for the vital sectors of the Channel coast from the Dutch-German border to the Loire. Later, the appointment of Col -General Blaskowitz to command Army Group G covering the Biscay and Mediterranean coasts of France, clearly, if unsatisfactorily, clarified the 'Ground Force Command'.

But the Ground Force Command, even in isolation, and it was virtually in isolation, remained subject to powerful influences, arising not only out of the divergencies of opinion between the C in C West and the Commander of Army Group B, but also from General Guderian,

Rommel, sharing Hitler's view that Normandy would be the main Allied target, and believing that the enemy must be annihilated, if possible on and in the sea, and certainly on the beaches, wanted the armour close up under his hand ready to deliver an immediate and massive counterstroke. He had had painful experience of Allied air supremacy in the Western Desert, and knew well the fate of armoured columns attempting to move by daylight under 'open-bomb sights'. If the armour was not there he doubted its ability to get there, and certainly not in time. It was, in any case, virtually impossible to move armour on the stricken roads by day.

Reminiscent of World War I. These
railway guns were the descendants of
Big Bertha, the gun which shelled
Paris

None doubted the magnitude of the
Allied air threat, of which they were
having daily and nightly experience,
but at the same time neither von
Rundstedt nor the Panzer Generals
agreed with Rommel's tactics, or
shared his beliefs about the site of
operations. First, von Rundstedt
visualised delivering massive counter-
strokes after the Allies had broken
through the outer crust of the sea
defences; secondly, he did not share
Rommel's views on Normandy; thirdly,
he could not agree to the commitment of the armoured reserve close
up before the event. The Air argument,
which rendered the armour difficult to
move, might easily trap it and destroy
it if Rommel had his way, and the
main assault should come in against
the Pas de Calais, or elsewhere.

Guderian, greatly worried about the
situation in both the East and West,
breakfasted alone with Hitler in early
January, 1944, and urged upon him the

necessity to strengthen the Eastern
defences and release much needed
reserves to the West. This touched off
a typical Hitler outburst:

'Believe me! I am the greatest
builder of fortifications of all time',
Hitler ranted. 'I built the West Wall;
I built the Atlantic Wall . . .' He then
began to deluge Guderian's ears with
'tons of concrete' and a mass of
statistics. In fact, Hitler had never
visited the 'Atlantic Wall', and it
existed largely in his imagination.

Guderian then toured the West, and
was at once alarmed by Rommel's
intended dispositions, and his intention to commit the Panzer Divisions
close up before the 'Day'. 'Disposed
thus', he wrote, 'they could not be
withdrawn and committed elsewhere
with sufficient rapidity'.

Back at Supreme Headquarters,
Guderian took the opportunity to
point out 'this error' in conference.
Hitler refused to countermand the
orders of the 'Man on the spot', and
advised Guderian to, 'Go to France
and discuss the matter once more with
Rommel'.

Guderian and von Geyr then visited

Rommel at his Headquarters at La Roche Guyon. The Field Marshal explained his views fully, but was not disposed to argue. Apart from his belief that Normandy would be the sector of assault, he was convinced that the enemy must be destroyed without gaining a foothold. Given his own way he might deliver such a blow to the enemy in the shallows and on the beaches that it would be impossible to mount a further assault, at least in that year. And if he were right in these beliefs, which he shared with Hitler, then he must be right about the disposition of the armour close up. The risk, admittedly was great, but there was no escape from that. Clearly Rommel did not share von Rundstedt's view that a battle of mobility might be won.

Hitler, meanwhile, clung to his intuitions, reinforced by his reasonable deductions from Allied troop placings, especially in the South-West of England, that Normandy would be the main target, and that

The men behind the guns . . .

Cherbourg would be the natural port for the Allies to aim at. But the nagging possibility of a second assault – even a major effort – elsewhere, began to divide his mind, disposing him far more than the commanders on the spot to the ultimate disasters of compromise.

Guderian had made a third attempt to convince Hitler of the dangers of Rommel's armoured dispositions, but early in May, Geyr von Schweppenburg, fearing that von Rundstedt was moving closer to Rommel's views, appealed to Hitler on his own account. He wanted to hold the bulk of his armour North and South of Paris, and at last Hitler dithered. The result was a disastrous compromise, whereby four Panzer Divisions were held as an assault reserve under the Command of OKW, Supreme Headquarters. This weakened Rundstedt's Command, for the old Field Marshal, already thwarted in his attempts to organise an Infantry reserve in Normandy by withdrawing strength from South of the Loire, now found himself deprived of the means to deliver an effective

counter-stroke against the beaches without seeking permission from OKW.

Thus von Geyr had unwittingly brought about a situation which was to prove fatal.

These were worries enough, but they were but one expression of a general weakness based on suspicion and decay at the top.

Whereas Rommel, in his natural desire to have full control of the battle his armies must fight, was in a position comparable with Montgomery's, von Rundstedt's position was not in any way comparable with Eisenhower's. Not only was von Rundstedt deprived of full control of his ground forces, but he was also forced to 'request' air and naval support when he might need them. There was no machinery for combined planning between the services. Worse, the Navy controlled the coastal batteries which must play a major part in repelling an assault. The fact that Naval and Air strength had been

the smaller U-boats in Atlantic ports were to be made available, but were not under his command.

In the event, even this small 'fleet' was virtually unable to put to sea.

The German 3rd Air Force, commanded by General Hugo Sperrle, was equally a broken reed. Compelled to use half-trained pilots its effectiveness, even with its dwindling numbers, was poor, and it was harried constantly on the ground as well as in the air. At the beginning of June 1944, the 3rd Air Force mustered some 400 aircraft operational 'on paper'. Again on paper these were divided between the 4th and 5th Fighter Divisions under 2nd Fighter Corps. Those under the 4th Division had the priority task of intercepting Allied bombers bound for the Reich, but could be diverted in the event of Allied assault landings. In the event neither the 2nd Air Corps, or its Divisions, had aircraft available to make their presence felt on the 'Day'. The promised Fighter 'Wings' on the way from Germany mostly

Rest period . . .

Drill

reduced to very small, almost negligible proportions, strengthened rather than weakened the need to co-operate and co-ordinate all available defences.

Admiral Theodor Krancke, C in C, German Naval Group West, had his small fleet of some sixty miscellaneous craft hemmed into port under incessant Allied air attack. Clashes in the Channel reduced his destroyer flotilla to two operational vessels. For the rest he could muster two torpedo boats, thirty-one motor torpedo boats, and a handful of patrol vessels and minesweepers. In addition fifteen of

failed to arrive. Few pilots knew France; few could read maps. The Chief of Staff of the 2nd Corps estimated that he had no more than fifty aircraft under command.

Thus, the Western Allies could not be challenged at sea or in the air, and Rommel had few illusions about his task. It was, in a sense, simple: the German Armies in the West, battered incessantly from the air, short of training, short of essential transport, and of poor quality, deprived by the disruption of their radar installations of the full use of their 'eyes' and 'ears', stood alone, waiting.

For nearly six months Field Marshal Rommel devoted his tremendous energies to the task of making the coastal defences impregnable from Cherbourg to the Somme, giving as much attention as was permitted to the problems of Normandy. Moved by a profound pessimism, untrammelled by the limitations of the orthodox military thinking which patterned the minds of von Rundstedt and the older school, perhaps even sub-consciously aware that there could be no compromise for Germany while Germany was Hitler, he knew that the enemy must be beaten on the beaches. Perhaps he knew also that it was a forlorn hope: there was no other.

There is no evidence to suggest that Rommel would have disliked a battle of manoeuvre. It was simply that he knew it would be too late, and lost. There was no room, therefore, for von Rundstedt's belief that the Allies were bound to gain a foothold, and that the battle for Normandy would then be fought. Gordon Harrison

commented in *Cross-Channel Attack:* 'The difference of opinion was essentially a difference in judgement of what was possible ... Rundstedt, like Sodenstern (Commanding the 19th Army), was clearly more optimistic...'

To Rommel such optimism was another name for despair, and Hitler, with the shadow of disaster already darkening his door, knew it also. Blumentritt remarked that messages from OKW at this time invariably began: 'The Führer fears ... '. He was full of fears, centring on Normandy where the Valkyrie rode the skies. But whereas Rommel was a realist concerned with men and materials, concrete and mines, guns and ammunition, Hitler was a visionary, seeing figures in a glass darkly. His support for Rommel was split too many ways, and never effective. He stated clearly, to Warlimont and others, that, 'If we do not stop the invasion and do not drive the enemy back into the sea, the war will be lost'. He had the greatest faith in Rommel, yet apart from ordering a few anti-tank and

anti-aircraft units to reinforce Western Normandy, he did almost nothing about it. US troop concentrations and assault landing exercises in South-West England pointed ever more clearly to Normandy and to Cherbourg, but Hitler vacillated. Neither he, nor anyone else, had conceived the possibility of the harbours the Allies planned to tow in their wake.

A powerful factor in the indecision in regard to the armoured reserve was the haunting fear that Normandy might not be the place, or only one place. The extreme lack of mobility of the German Armies in the West haunted the minds of the Commanders. The Allied Air Forces would not only be able, in Rommel's considered opinion, to prevent troop movement in battle, but they had already knocked the wheels from under the ground troops, condemning them to static rôles.

It was impossible to make the best of it. In spite of repeated demands Rommel did not receive the command control essential to the carrying out of his basic plans even on a minimum basis. His demands for labour and materials could not be 'orders', but merely 'requests' through the normal channels. Denied the help of the Todt Organisation, fully extended on fortress work mainly in the Pas de Calais, and unable to cope with the sustained Allied air attacks which were wrecking the transport services, Rommel used his troops as labourers to the detriment of their essential training. Some units were employed for three full days a week on labouring tasks, and much of the remainder of their time was taken up with special guard duties.

In February, Rommel issued a directive to his army commanders, and repreated it again towards the end of April:

'In the short time left before the great offensive starts, we must succeed in bringing all defences to such a standard that they will hold up against the strongest attacks. Never in history was there a defence of such an extent with such an obstacle as the sea. The enemy must be annihilated before he reaches our main battle-field. We must stop him in the water, not only delaying him but destroying all his equipment while it is still afloat'.

Repeatedly he emphasised to his commanders and staff that the first twenty-four hours would be decisive. He conceived an elaborate system of obstacles between high and low water marks covering the beaches, which would make the passage even of flat bottomed boats perilous in the extreme, if not impossible. He planned to lay 50 million mines as the first line of sea defence, and sow minefields over the beaches. The mines were never available, and when at last inadequate deliveries were made, the minelayers were immobilised by Allied air attack and unable to put to sea. In the event not more than six million mines were laid, little more than one-tenth of the minimum programme.

Regarding von Rundstedt's 'Zweite Stellung' or second line of defence as 'a waste of time', Rommel ordered all work upon it to cease, and the entire effort concentrated upon strengthening the forward positions. Innumerable 'hedgehogs' and anti-tank obstacles were moved forward to reinforce the massive concoctions of angle iron, the 'Tetrahydra' and 'Belgian Gates', which with thousands of mined stakes slanted seaward, mazed the approaches to the beaches. So grave was the shortage of labour that the 352nd Division, covering the vital stretch of beach from Grandcamp to Arromanches had to cut and haul its own stakes from the Cerisy forest, eleven miles inland, and drive each stake by hand into position.

In the areas behind the Cotentin, Rommel had planned an extensive network of poles linked by wires and mined as a defence in depth against airborne landings. When the work should have been completed in the middle of May he visited the site and found that the task was only in its opening stages. The 13,000 shells necessary to set off explosions were not available.

The acute shortage of labour, mines and materials of all kinds, and the reduction of transport to the horse and cart and the bicycle, made the

Men and concrete; the dragon's teeth behind the main wall

61

carrying out of a massive defensive plan impossible. Of ten million mines needed for the 30-mile front of the 352nd Division only ten thousand were forthcoming, and these did not include any 'Teller' mines. The situation of the 716th and 711th Divisions covering the vital frontage behind the Normandy beaches was no better. Not more than two-thirds of the coastal guns covering the Army Group front had been casemated by the end of May. A system of strong points spaced from eight hundred to thirteen hundred yards apart were in the main unprotected. 'Of the installations in the sector of the 352nd Division only 15 per cent were bombproof; the remainder were virtually unprotected from air attack', wrote Gordon Harrison. The 716th Division regarded its situation as even worse.

The minimum daily need of the 7th Army in Normandy to fulfill its construction tasks was for 240 carloads of cement alone. In one typical three-day period the records show that it received 47 carloads. The forced closure of the Cherbourg cement works for lack of coal aggravated the extreme shortage. This was, above all, due to the Allied attacks on road and rail transport.

These desperate shortages sharpened the edge of Rommel's bitter criticism of the Luftwaffe. He pointed out that the Luftwaffe employed 50,000 men to maintain its communications, and engaged a further 300,000 on ground services. This worked out at 100 men on the ground to every man in the air. That Hugo Sperrle, commanding the 3rd Air Force, largely shared his views availed nothing. The situation existed to feed the grandiose dreams of Göring.

Rommel's repeated attempts to gain the services of the 3rd Flak Corps in Normandy were thwarted, and it remained under the 3rd Air Force, subject to the whims of Göring, and useless in defence. It might have done much to counter the overwhelming air strength of the Allies, and would have given some comfort and a sense of 'hitting back' to the battered troops in their dug-outs. Even the 2nd Parachute Corps, tactically under 7th Army, remained administratively and for training under the Luftwaffe.

Göring refused to permit these troops to be used to help in defence works.

Thus, as June opened, the gaps in the defences were frightful. Each new device had been observed by the Allies, and often tested through the courage of the small teams of men who explored the shallows by night. By abandoning the 'Zweite Stellung' the defences had been deprived of depth, and reduced to an outer crust too fragile to withstand the immense weight of assault in store for it. Nevertheless, the fault was not Rommel's. He had attempted the impossible, and had achieved much. He had inherited a myth, and had given it 'teeth' to inflict a dangerous, if not deadly, bite. He had also greatly improved the dispositions of his troops.

On the eve of 'D day', Field Marshal von Rundstedt's Command in the West numbered 60 divisions, one of them, the 19th Panzer Division, re-fitting after a severe hammering on the Eastern Front, another in the Channel Islands, reduced the effective total to 58 divisions.

Of these, 31 divisions were in static rôles, and 27, including 10 armoured divisions, were as mobile as the suspicions of the Führer and the available resources allowed. They were disposed from Holland to the Atlantic and Mediterranean coasts, 5 divisions in Holland in the 88th Corps, including the 'lame' 19th Panzer, 19 in the Pas de Calais between the Scheldt and the Seine, 18 between the Seine and the Loire. The remainder were south of the Loire.

43 divisions out of the grand total of 60 were grouped under Field Marshal Rommel's Army Group B, the 88th Corps in Holland, the powerful 15th Army in the Pas de Calais, the 7th Army in Normandy. The 15th Army commanded by von Salmuth was virtually anchored in its positions, mainly by the incapability of the German military mind to disengage itself from a pre-conceived idea. The Western Allies did their best to nurture the illusion.

By the eve of 'D day', Field Marshal Rommel had succeeded in improving and strengthening the dispositions of the 7th Army under Dollmann which,

Practice alert

he believed, must fight the decisive battle on the beaches. The 352nd and 716th Infantry Divisions lay in their dug-outs and resistance 'nests' along the coast of Calvados from the Vire river to the Orne. On the German left flank the 91st Division, with the 6th Parachute Regiment under command, covered the left flank of the 352nd in the area of Carentan. The 709th Division covered the Eastern coastline of the Cherbourg Peninsula. Behind its right flank positions, known to the Allies by the code name 'Utah' beach, the extensive marshes and the flooded areas following the courses of the rivers Dives and Merderet from Carentan to le Port Brehay, were regarded as safeguarding the rear, and blocking the exits from the beaches. The 243rd Division faced west in the Peninsula.

On the German right flank the 711th Division with one regiment of the 346th Division under command covered the coast from the river Orne to the Seine Estuary opposite le Havre.

The 709th, the 352nd and the 716th

Infantry Divisions would, therefore, meet the Allied assaults on the beaches code named 'Utah', 'Omaha', 'Gold', 'Juno', 'Sword'. Against the will of von Rundstedt, Rommel had succeeded in bringing up the 21st Panzer Division to the Caen area, poised to strike against the Allied left flank. The three armoured divisions, the 12th and 116th Panzer, and the Panzer Lehr, the Army Group B reserve, capable of delivering a massive punch, lay in the rectangle Mantes-Gassicourt, Chartres, Bernay, Gacé, the 116th forward. But the fears of von Rundstedt, Guderian and von Geyr had placed the force under OKW, subject to the will of Hitler. Thus, the outcome of the day of decision lay with the coastal batteries and with the three divisions entrenched along the Normandy coast, the 91st Division and its Parachute Regiment on the left, and the 21st Panzer Division on the right. If these should fail to hold and destroy the Allies in the shallows and on the beaches the fate of Nazi Germany would be sealed, and in the pattern of the remaining days the future of

Europe would be formed.

The Allied assault had been expected in the middle of May, and in spite of warnings from the German Naval Command in the West, the military view was that the assault would be at high tide. When the middle of May had safely passed there was a tendency to relax, in the belief that the attempt would be delayed until August. Enemy appreciations continued to be governed by the belief that the Allies must gain the use of a port or ports, and Naval opinion moved away from the Pas de Calais, hardening in the belief that Le Havre and Cherbourg would be the main objectives. Allied troops and shipping concentrations in the south and south-west of England strongly supported this view, as also did the comparative freedom of the two ports from air attack, and the general pattern of Allied bombing at the end of May. The Navy also believed that the rocky shallows covering the eastern sector of the Normandy coast would rule out landings, and expected that a major effort would come in against the Cotentin, together with airborne landings.

By the end of May, Admiral Krancke, Navy Group West, had lulled himself into an optimism, the more remarkable in view of the almost total immobilisation of his Naval force. He believed that his coastal batteries could blow the Allied Armada out of the water, and noted that Allied air attacks on the batteries had accounted for only eight guns, five of them between Le Havre and Le Treport, and three in Normandy. The Admiral began to believe that the massed shipping in British ports, the immense activities, the assault exercises, of which the enemy had some knowledge from isolated air reconnaissance and the reports of agents, were all part of a gigantic bluff. In effect he plumped for 'Rankin C', the Allied plan to move in as the Germans moved out.

The rapid deterioration of the weather in the first days of June ruled out the possibility of invasion in the mind of the enemy. The interceptions of warning messages broadcast to the Resistance and handed to Admiral Dönitz, failed to weigh against the high winds and rising seas in the Channel. On the 4th June, while

General Eisenhower met with his Admirals, Air Marshals, Generals and weather forecasters at Portsmouth, and the approaches to the Channel already seethed with the ships of the spearhead troops, Admiral Krancke in Normandy reached the view that no attack was or could be imminent. General Blumentritt, Chief of Staff, OB West agreed with him.

In the shallows off shore the midget submarines of Lieut Honour watched and waited. All the US Force U and a proportion of Force O had sailed, and at nine o'clock on the morning of the 4th June, Force U2a of 128 Tank Landing craft was 25 miles south of St Catherine's Point, having failed to receive the message of postponement following the decision of the Supreme Commander in the early hours. Two destroyers and a Walrus aircraft were anxiously heading Force U2a before it showed up on the enemy radar screens. Throughout the day the Force plunged back striving to make the shelter of Weymouth Bay against fierce head winds and a high sea.

Throughout the night of the 31st May, 830 buoys had been laid by the HDML's of Force J, and on the 4th June the buoys had begun to transmit signals. At six o'clock on the evening of the 4th June, Royal Navy HDML's were marking the buoyed channels for the passage of the assault ships and their escorts. Ten approach channels had been swept clear of mines by all available mine-sweeping flotillas.

At fifteen minutes to ten o'clock on the night of the 4th June, General Eisenhower reached his final decision that the assault should go in on the morning of the 6th, and the vast array of ships and assault craft began to move out of its ports and estuaries, its shelters and anchorages towards the rendezvous just south of the Isle of Wight, to sail thence to its tryst with destiny.

Had invisible forces of the planet Mars massed against them, the enemy could have been scarcely less aware. Its once great Air Force, which had threatened to rule the skies, had no longer eyes to see. The elaborate warning systems and radar installations, battered by bombs and jammed by a maze of electronic interference, failed to warn of danger impending.

The U boat fleets which had made of the broad Atlantic a death trap and a burial ground, and reduced the Arctic seas to a narrow desperate gauntlet, were sunk or confined under concrete bays. The 'secret' weapons conceived in its workshops had been hunted down like rats and forced into holes in the rocky hills.

Yet such facts as these serve not only as a measure of the Nazi weakness, but of its great remaining strength. Vast armies still sprawled over all Europe from the Arctic Ocean to the Black Sea, and from the Mediterranean, Biscay and Channel coasts to the North Cape. Black smoke still poured from the chimneys of its human incinerators, and countless thousands, not only in Nazi Germany, but in Holland and France, suffered the appalling torments of its concentration camps. This was the enemy.

On the morning of the 5th June, Field Marshal Rommel, re-assured by the reports of the meteorological experts – for the enemy was deprived even of essential meteorological data – left by motor car for his home at Ulm on the Danube. It was deemed unsafe for senior commanders to travel by air.

Sea-front into defence point; the houses have been evacuated and bunkers built below. Note the painted handrail

Before the dawn

Sunrise at two minutes to six o'clock on the morning of 5th June, 1944, was an arbitrary statement rather than a visible fact marking the progress from dark stormy night to grey blustery day. The Channel heaved in a chaos of cruel pinnacles flecked white upon steel grey, and waves rose steeply to test the seamanship and try the stomachs of all those afloat in little ships. Clouds fled in tormented tattered shrouds over a cold sky. A gusty westerly, veering WSW to WNW at Force 5, whipped the spume into the faces of look-outs and helmsmen as scores of small craft reared and bucked towards their meeting place. By sunrise five thousand ships of half-a-hundred shapes and sizes had begun to move from their anchorages, and the wakes of many convoys already patterned the coastal waters of Britain from Fowey to the Nore. It was four years almost to the day since the remnants of an army had struggled back from Dunkirk, and the coastal waters of England had known any comparable activity. Admiral Ramsay had commanded then, and he commanded now, on this morning. The memory was a source of secret pride to many again on the waters, and from it they gained strength and resolution.

This 5th day of June is not one of those landmarks in history to be covered by easy generalisation. It was many things to many men. 287,000 men and a host of armoured fighting vehicles had been pre-loaded into ships, some of them since the first day of the month, some of them had been already shuttled and shunted, blind to sea and sky, daylight or darkness, sick, weary, wondering, aware that a moment would come when they would be spewed up like Jonahs upon an alien shore, bristling with devices of death and beaten with shot and shell. Yet it was a moment to be wished for; an end.

The many thousands on deck, however sick and cold, could count themselves fortunate that they were not of the many thousands below, huddled in the great caverns of the LCT's, in the cramped quarters of the LSI's, in the dull yellow electric glow, and the stench of vomit. Even those with strong stomachs were overcome.

The Invasion Fleet in stern order and arrangement, lying off the English coast ready for the assault

While thousands waited in a grey limbo, thousands worked, manning the little ships and the great ships of war, alert in hundreds of gun turrets, crouched astride swivel seats behind a great array of weapons pointing to the sky, cloud ceiling 4,000 feet, and above that the sustained roar of ten thousand aircraft. Hundreds more wrestled with towing gear and hawsers,

tugs grappling and towing strange ungainly shapes out of the estuaries in the wake of the Armada massing south of the Isle of Wight. It would be a grim day and a grim night for tows, and hundreds of tons of concrete and steel would break loose to wallow in the steep seas.

Towards evening there was a break in the weather, and in that brief hour a soldier wrote: 'It was a perfect summer's evening, the Isle of Wight lay green and friendly, and tantalisingly peaceful behind the tapestry of war-

ships.' The men were answering cheer with cheer across the water, the pennants flew from the ships of war, and a British Admiral threw his cap in the air.

Yet what a travesty of the truth this is to the thousands who seemed to inhabit a grey ante-chamber to a morgue, to whom the measurement of time had become almost meaningless, dull sickness upon them to eke out the miseries of the long blind ordeal of waiting.

Force U2a, part of Force U for 'Utah', had had the worst of it: 128 Tank Landing Craft crowded with men and armour, sailing out of the west through the hours of indecision, easting down Channel, turned about, and plunging back into the teeth of the westerly to seek shelter in Weymouth Bay and in the Lea of Portland, easting again down Channel, at last in the dusk of 5th June to set course south for France.

Force O for 'Omaha' had had also a long haul from the south-west, a turn and turn-about, an agonising drawing out of the hours of confinement. Already men on deck had kept watch upwards of fifty hours, and perhaps fifty more lay ahead before sleep. For these no cheers, no happy vision of the Isle of Wight, for their 'green and pleasant land' lay beyond the Atlantic.

Through the hours of darkness the immense convoys moved steadily, unmolested, on their courses in the buoyed channels cleared by the minesweeping flotillas, a wedge more than fifty miles wide, and with scores of small fighting ships ranging far out on the flanks probing for the enemy. There was nothing. The long lines of ships seemed to unwind on fabulous spools, drawing their component threads from a hundred havens of the English coast, to weave them into thick skeins to the Bay of Seine. The fierce turbulence of wind and sea failed to mask the strange 'unnatural' silence of the night. The sustained thunder of the fleets of bombers overhead, quenched for those below by the drenching sounds of sea, and the

On the way at last

shuddering stresses of steel plates, seemed to accentuate the absence of the enemy.

While many marvelled, few drew comfort, for how could it be possible that such an avalanche of ships and men could muster through the months, at last to fill the English Channel from shore to shore, and remain undetected? Surely no instrument more 'scientific' than the human ear would be needed to hear so vast a throb of power.

Before the sun had set on the evening of the 5th, two flotillas of minesweepers stood off the coast of Normandy, well within sight, and easily able to distinguish houses on shore with the naked eye. The Midget Submarines of Lieut. Honour's command were at their stations, close inshore marking the Eastern flank and the dangerous rocks. There were no signs of detection. From two o'clock in the morning of the 6th, the Headquarters ships of the assault moved into their transport areas, and prepared to put their assault craft into the water. The only interference

came from the unfriendly sea. The weather was not alone to thank, or blame, for this.

The sustained attacks from the air on the elaborate Early Warning System of the enemy had succeeded almost too well. In the entire 'Neptune' Area from Cap d'Antifer to Barfleur, 74 radar stations were out of action, and the 18 still capable of working were silent. But it was not enough simply to blind the enemy it was important also to mislead. For this purpose 10 stations were deliberately left in working order north of the Seine, and on to these screens the Royal Navy contrived to produce a misleading web of shapes and echoes. It seems extravagant that such a claim is made, for it reveals a predominance over the enemy that reduces his forces to a stricken body, lacerated on all sides, unable to fly or float, but capable of inflicting grievous, even crippling, wounds upon those seeking to deliver the *coup de grace*.

But there was no inclination on the part of the Allies to under-estimate the powers of the German Army in the West. Thus all through the 5th June and the night, 105 aircraft of the RAF and 34 little ships of the Royal Navy contrived by means of weaving patterns over the sky and sea, and flying barrage balloons, to produce the 'echoes' in the enemy radar ears of a substantial fleet approaching the Pas de Calais. At the same time jamming operations and diversions were carried on against Cap d'Antifer and Barfleur. The silent approach of the great Armada to spread out in a fan from eight to twelve miles off shore enclosing the Bay of Seine is the measure of success.

Soon after nine o'clock, the unusual length and content of the BBC broadcast warning to the French Resistance alarmed the enemy, and the 15th Army in the Pas de Calais was alerted, while the 7th Army in Normandy remained undisturbed. Nothing, it seemed, could prise von Rundstedt's mind away from its pre-conceived fixations, even the deadly facts of elements of three airborne divisions

Air strike on the way

dropping in the midst of his forces. Well before the first assault craft of the seaborne forces were in the water the battle on land was joined.

Within half-an-hour of sunset on the night of the 5th June, while the leading ships of the seaborne assault moved into the buoyed channels to steer for France, the Pathfinders of the United States and British Air Forces took off from their English fields to light their beacons in the fields of Normandy. Soon after midnight these small vanguards of elite troops were moving silently in the midst of the enemy, the British to mark the dropping zones for the 6th

Below: Into the landing craft.
Right: The last leg into the beaches

Airborne Division to the north-east of Caen on the eastern flank, the Americans astride the Merderet river, and the road Carentan-Montebourg-Cherbourg in the area of St Mére Eglise. Behind them more than 1,200 aircraft bore nearly 20,000 men into battle; behind them the gliders for which paratroops must clear the way.

It was an operation that had filled Air Marshal Sir Trafford Leigh-Mallory with forebodings. He feared very high casualties, especially for the large Western Forces, but his doubts and fears had been over-ridden. The

Airborne assault must go in. The Supreme Commander had not been without misgivings, and on the night of the 5th he stayed with the 101st US Airborne Division until after midnight, when the last aircraft was in the air. He felt the better for it. He had found the men 'in fine fettle', expressing themselves full of confidence.

Leigh-Mallory, making the rounds of as many airfields as possible, sought to satisfy himself that all possible had been done to give the men a good chance. Many had never before experienced flak, and the difficulties and delays in obtaining sufficient numbers of transport aircraft had left training short of the highest standards to be wished for. The same applied to the crews of the tank landing craft at sea, and for the same reasons. Yet at sea there may be often a second, even a third chance while in the air a man seldom has more than 'one life'.

Would their training see them – and their cargoes – safely through to the dropping zones? Only the night would yield an answer. At least all had been well briefed and rehearsed.

Leigh-Mallory had no touchstone

whereby to judge the temper of the Americans, but of his own men he wrote that their demeanour was 'grim and not frightfully gay, but there was no doubt in my mind of their determination to do the job.' Another who watched the 7th Battalion of the British 5th Parachute Brigade in the hour before take-off noted the 'sombre and determined mood', the complete absence of exaggerated high spirits, no joking, some quiet singing, and a 'certain amount of honest funk.'

The last warning of the Brigadier commanding the British 3rd Parachute Brigade may well serve for all:

'Do not be daunted if chaos reigns: it undoubtedly will.'

Above: Off-shore cruiser; USS Augusta. *Right:* Early casualties; hit landing craft towed out of danger area

75

The airborne: the western flank

The drop of the US 101st Airborne Division, as fully plotted as all subsequent information has made possible, spatters the map over an area twenty-five miles long by fifteen miles broad, and with small isolated elements even further afield. Very few of these had even an outside chance of becoming part of the Division. The men had been loosed, as it seems, recklessly upon the winds of Heaven, and thence to the flooded hinterlands, and maze of closed country, behind 'Utah' beach.

The 82nd Division, largely due to the arrival of one regiment reasonably on its objectives, was a little better, but of the remainder of the Division only four per cent were dropped in their zones west of the Merderet river.

Thus the tasks of the Division west of the Merderet, and the crossings of the Merderet and Douve rivers, could not be fulfilled or secured. The Division had become a Regiment.

At dawn, when the seaborne landings were coming in on 'Utah' beach, the 101st Division mustered 1,100 men out of 6,600. By evening its strength had grown to 2,500 men. The 82nd Division, at least 4,000 men short on the day, was still only at one-third strength three days later. Both divisions had lost great quantities of equipment,

Left : Eisenhower talks with the men before take-off. *Below :* US glider-borne take-off. *Bottom :* US paratroopers en route

Left: First wave down. *Below:* First casualties: eight men died when the Horsa crashed. *Above:* German soldiers cautiously inspect the first debris of invasion

and almost their entire glider-borne artillery, much of it in the floods of the Merderet and Douve rivers. Neither division was able to prepare adequately for the arrival of its glider-borne follow up, and losses were severe and tragic.

Yet the remarkable fact is that so great a confusion was created in the enemy by this incoherent scattering of men into their midst that there was no possibility of reserves supporting the beach defenders, or the means of substantial counter attack. By the time the US 4th Infantry Division came in to land the battle of 'Utah' beach was virtually won.

No coherent pattern has ever emerged from the struggles of the isolated remnants of the Airborne Divisions on that day; nor will such a pattern ever emerge. The individual contributions of many men who fought bravely alone or in twos and threes

will never be assessed. Even those who gave up without a fight added to rather than subtracted from enemy bewilderment. The Pathfinders of the Airborne did not do well. Many failed to find and to mark the dropping zones; some beacons were missing entirely, especially west of the Merderet in country infested by enemy; others were wrongly placed. Pilots under fire for the first time, many of them 'inadequately briefed', took wild evasive action, lost direction in the cloud banks, and overshot the dropping zones. Many came in too fast and too high, and spilled out their 'sticks' of men, adding greatly to the normal hazards of jumping.

Major-General Maxwell Taylor, Commanding the 101st, dropped within a nucleus of his Divisional Headquarters, and struggled all through the day to make contact and to bring some sort of order out of chaos. Nevertheless, he felt 'alone on the Cotentin' through most of the day.

In fact, the unpredictable mixture of the docile and the devilish dropping in ones and twos into his lap, paralysed the enemy, and the very wildness

79

of the drop became the most potent factor in its strange success. It seemed to the enemy that he was beset on all sides by hosts of vague shadows, materialising at a number of seemingly disconnected points into the harsh black reality of desperate bands of men. He had no means of assessing the numbers arrayed against him, or the directions from which to expect attacks. The disruption of his communications made it difficult at best, and more often impossible, to add together the small fragments of the puzzle collecting in the hands of battalions, regiments and outposts. He was more 'lost' than his adversary, and aware as never before that he was in an alien land, and with every hand ready to turn against him.

By a stroke of remarkable fortune a small band of men ambushed and killed the commander of the German 91st Division, returning from an 'Exercise' conference to his headquarters. Thus the 91st Division, trained in the rôle of defence against airborne attack, and forming almost the sole available reserve behind the defenders of the Cotentin coast, was deprived of its commander, and severely handicapped. There was no 'shape' or dimension to the airborne enemy, no focal point or points to counter-attack, no time to think, no commander with the temerity to commit troops with the strength and purpose of knowledge.

Many small villages in the coastal areas had been organised as strong points, and in these villages the German garrisons were as isolated and lonely as those who attacked them haphazard out of the night. Enemy regimental commanders, listening anxiously to the growing overtones of war in the sky, were at times overwhelmed. Reports reaching the German 7th Army, and Army Group B, failed to produce coherent patterns on the operations maps. Too much and too little was known. Nothing fitted together. From Caen in the east almost to the western shores of the Cotentin, airborne landings were reported, while from the air in the early hours deluges of bombs fell upon the beaches and the forward defensive positions.

And at last the seaborne Armada began to put its multitude of men and landing craft into the water off the Normandy coast. While many were sure that this must be the beginning of the main Allied assault, so long awaited and expected, and that the battlefield was Normandy, others, including Lieut-General Speidel, Rommel's Chief of Staff, and Lieut.-General Blumentritt, Chief of Staff to von Rundstedt, were doutbful. Thus the German military machine remained hesistant and palsied, its slender reserves uncommitted, its armour waiting, Rommel out of touch, Hitler sleeping. These things gave the troops on the western flank an initial advantage of which, perforce, they were unaware, and saved them from the possibility of annihilation.

The primary tasks of the 101st Division were to seize and hold the western exits of the four causeways over the floods behind 'Utah' beach, and extending from St Germain-de-Varreville to Pouppeville. To the south they had to seize the La Barquette lock, which controlled the river level, and establish bridgeheads across the Douve below Carentan. Thus they would open the way through for the seaborne troops, secure the southern flank of VII Corps, and be ready to link-up with V Corps assaulting at 'Omaha'.

Less than an hour after the first of the paratroopers began to hurtle down from the weaving aircraft, six distinguishable columns composed of miscellaneous elements of the Division had begun to move upon the objectives. Each column had at its head a Colonel or Lieut-Colonel, and by the act of moving in an orderly and deliberate manner on a definite purpose, each column added 'lost' individuals to its strength.

The remarkable chance of a bundle jammed in the doorway of his aircraft delayed the jump of Colonel Johnson and a load of men, bringing them

The Utah Bombardment. *Top left:* U.S. Naval guns pound the beach.
Top right: 14-inch guns of USS Nevada blast the defences.
Middle left: 20-mm gun in close support. *Middle right:* Broadside from USS Nevada. *Bottom:* RAF Mitchells go in

Top left: Ramps down; the men go in.
Bottom left: Surprise and the shattering bombardment allowed some to drive ashore in comfort. *Above and right:* At Utah the build-up proceeds, untroubled by calamity. *Below:* By the end of the day at Utah, even a road had been laid

down within reach of the La Barquette lock. Mustering a total force 150 strong, Johnson moved swiftly on the lock, detaching fifty men to rush the position. The party were across before the enemy reacted with mortar fire and shelling. At best it was a slender bridgehead, and no more than one hundred yards in depth, but Colonel Johnson had to take chances. Patrols told him that he was in the midst of a confusion of enemy and small pockets of his own troops. In spite of many brave attempts the Douve bridges and the southern flank remained unsecured.

Meanwhile five Colonels were moving with varying speeds and fortunes upon the urgent tasks of seizing the beach exits. None knew of the existence of the others. Each column was entirely on its own, aiming at what might be possible and of the greatest importance.

A few miles to the south, near the village of Culoville, a Regimental Commander had been striving since long before the dawn to establish a Regimental Command post, and serve as a focal point for his regiment. Harassed on all sides the Colonel was often hard put to it to maintain a precarious position; nevertheless, he had sent his only possible 'reserve', a force of fifty men, under the only one of his battalion commanders with whom he was able to make contact, to secure the southern beach exit at Pouppeville. Urging this force to make all possible speed the Colonel suffered a loneliness which he quite wrongly believed to be unique in the Cotentin Peninsula.

At the same hour a Colonel with two hundred men was struggling south upon the same mission. He had been dropped miles to the north of his objective.

Perhaps fortunately General Taylor knew nothing of these moves. He had managed to establish the nucleus of a divisional command post in some strength, but all beyond that was a closed book. He at once ordered a force of fifty men to march on Pouppeville, and joined the march himself with eighteen officers. Thus three independent columns converged on the southern exits.

It was eight o'clock when this small force reached Pouppeville, blooded its nose on the enemy outposts, and unable to manoeuvre, fought bitterly from house to house. At noon, when the the remains of the German garrison surrendered, pressed also by the leading Infantry of the 4th Division from the causeway, the force had lost eighteen men.

Meanwhile, a second column reached Houdienville in time to find the sea-borne forces streaming through. The third force had made even slower progress, unable to shake loose from small groups of enemy harassing *his* flanks.

Throughout the whole day and the night the 101st Division, reduced to much less effective strength than a regiment, was not only isolated from its own widely scattered units, but also in complete ignorance of the fate of the 82nd.

The story of the 82nd Division is simple. Two of its regiments with the tasks of clearing the area west of the Merderet river and the angle of the Douve, were not in the fight. It fell to one regiment to save the day, and to fight the one clear-cut battle fought by the US Airborne Forces on 'D day'. While scores of men struggled in the swamps of the Merderet, dragging themselves towards the dry land of the railway embankment, concerned in the main with the problem of survival, the third regiment had dropped in a fairly tight group to the north-west of St. Mére Eglise. This was not due to chance, but to the determination of the pilots, as widely scattered as all the rest, to find their targets. Long before the dawn, a battalion commander, finding himself on the outskirts of St. Mére Eglise with roughly a quarter of his battalion, bounced the town without waiting for more, or bothering with the slow and deadly business of house to house clearance. Taking the enemy completely by surprise he began to establish a solid base, which must prove of inestimable value.

By the afternoon the town was securely held, and four recognisable actions had developed, apart from a

Utah Beach from the air as the men swarm up the beach

score or more of fragmentary encounters in the hopeless wilderness west of the Merderet.

The 82nd had dropped on the fringe of the assembly area of the German 91st Division, and its position from the outset was much more precarious than that of the 101st. All troops, however fragmentary, were at once in the midst of the enemy, and fighting for their lives within minutes of finding their feet. Some small groups up to fifty or sixty strong fought all day in the ditches and hedgerows within one thousand yards of others with whom it was impossible to make contact. Often they were unaware of their nearness. At the same time, General Gavin, Second-in-Command of the Division, dredged the fields and swamps for men and equipment, and at last began to move with a recognisable force south along the railway embankment to join in the attack

Buried alive by the bombardment, a German soldier digs his way out to captivity

Top left: Survivors from a hit
landing-craft come ashore.
Bottom left: Mass held on the
beachhead. *Top right:* Inland, U.S. troops
cross flooded fields. *Bottom right:* Second
wave gliders going in

The inevitable price . . .

against La Fière from the east.

But these were forlorn hopes, harassing an enemy off balance, yet fighting with resolution, and greatly outnumbering the airborne troops.

Meanwhile, to the north astride the main road Carentan to Montebourg, a platoon, forty-two men strong, with two 57mm. anti tank guns and a few bazookas, moved unmolested through Neuville and reached the high ground immediately to the north. Hardly were the men deployed when the enemy attacked from the north. Harassed by intense mortar fire, and constantly assaulted by infantry outnumbering the platoon by at least five to one, every man held firm. At last ,in the evening, sixteen men withdrew steadily through Neuville, leaving twenty-six men of their platoon dead on the hillside. They had safeguarded St. Mère Eglise from counter-attack from the north for eight hours.

The performance of the 101st and 82nd Airborne Divisions on 'D day' must be seen in such fragmentary terms as these. The bewilderment their widespread drop created in the enemy was perhaps, of greater effect

than would have been possible if a had gone according to plan. At th end of the day the Divisions had no made contact. Each believed it ha lost some two-thirds of its troop Neither one had cause for satisfactio or the haziest idea of what was happen ing. All that they could do was t wait for the morning.

In fact, the enemy's confusion wa equivalent to almost total break down. Hammered savagely and in cessantly from the air, handicappe by the chance of a conference a Rennes of their Senior Commander their communications disrupted, an with, as it seems, a premonition c inevitable doom, their resistance wa as fragmentary as that of the airborn troops infesting their imaginations a well as their fields. Many surrendere almost without a fight. Major von de Heydte, commanding the German 6t Parachute Regiment, probably th finest enemy troops available in th Carentan area, has told of his difficu ties in getting orders from his Senic Commanders. From the church steepl of St Côme-du-Mont he had a person view of the Armada on the wester

Left: The first prisoners are brought in, some incredibly young. *Above:* The first prison-cage. *Right:* First signs of counterattack. *Below:* The airborne forces, inland, settle into a French chateau

flank. It seemed to him curiously detached from reality, almost peaceful. At noon the sun was shining, and the whole scene reminded him 'of a summer's day on the Wannsee'. The immense bustle of landing craft, and the warships fading into the horizon, lacked to his ears the orchestration of battle.

Von der Heydte sent his three battalions into battle, one to the north to attack St Mère Eglise, another to the north-east to protect the seaward flank in the area St. Marie-du-Mont, the third back on Carentan. Von der Heydte almost at once lost contact. Organised defence on the western flank had crumbled like the Walls of Jericho.

93

The sea behind them

94

At two o'clock on the morning of the 6th June, the leading ships of Force U, organised in twelve convoys comprising 865 vessels commanded by Rear Admiral Moon, USN, moved into their assembly area twelve miles off the western coast of the Cotentin Peninsular, opposite the Dunes of Vareville, 'Utah' beach.

Within six hours, three distinct assaults from the sea would go in upon the 50-mile stretch of Normandy coast, linked by the common factor of the Naval Operation 'Neptune'. Meticulous planning and attention to detail brought the great warships, the bombarding squadrons, the landing ships, the innumerable assault craft and their close supporting vessels,

safely through ten mine-swept channels to their marker ships off shore. In the last hour an immense fire plan would attempt to blast the troops through the enemy beach defences. The success of each assault would be vital to the development of a common bridgehead from which the 'Overlord' plan for the defeat of Germany could bring decisive defeat. There the wedge must be driven in, and held against the full force of enemy armour until such time as the right and centre could develop its strength.

Failure at 'Omaha', the western centre, would expose a dangerous flank, but if the eastern wedge held, the position might be repaired.

The assault upon 'Utah' beach, the extreme western flank, was on that day virtually an isolated operation. If all else failed it might have been reinforced to establish a bridgehead, to cut off the Cotentin Peninsula, gaining Cherbourg as a major port from which to mount some subsequent effort. In that event 'Overlord' would be no more.

Field Order No 1 states:
'VII Corps assaults 'Utah' beach on 'D day' at H hour and captures Cherbourg with minimum delay.'

At half-past two o'clock the Headquarter Ship, *Bayfield*, of Force U anchored at her station. It was a bad morning for small craft. A westerly wind blowing at fifteen knots whipped the choppy seas into waves three feet high. The cloud ceiling had risen to 11,900 feet, with low scuds of cloud at 1 to 5,000 feet. Four or five miles inshore the arm of the Cotentin gave some shelter, but the US Naval Commanders, submitted grudgingly to British Command, and rejected Admiral Ramsay's advice to assemble not more than eight miles off shore. They held the view that it would be dangerously close to the shore batteries, but in fact alien command was intolerable, and many could not conceal their 'intense personal and professional distaste', as Ingersoll remarked. Admiral King had given them a clear lead.

Now, at any rate, they were on their own, and there was no interference from any cause other than the wind and sea. A handful of enemy E-boats had turned back into Cherbourg,

Top left & left: The assault wave goes in on Omaha. *Above:* View from the beach

having failed to make contact. The Isles of Marcouf, which might have been manned as an observation post, were occupied by a detachment of US Cavalry Troops 132 strong. Four men armed with knives had swum ashore at half-past four o'clock, and found the islands deserted.

Steadily in the hours before dawn the orders to VII Corps reduced down to those few who would debouch into the shallows of the unfriendly sea. The 4th Infantry Division would establish the bridgehead; the 8th Infantry Regiment leading, the 1st battalion on the right, 'Green beach', the 2nd battalion on the left, 'Red beach', two companies of each battalion forward, thirty men to each landing craft, five landing craft to each company, twenty landing craft carrying six hundred men in the van, with two companies of the 70th Tank Battalion in the first wave. Behind them, wave upon wave of their fellows and the waves of the sea, H plus 5, H

plus 15, H plus 17, H plus 30, on and on through all the day and night, and beyond; infantry, armour, engineers, into the shallows, through the obstacles, the mine-fields, over the beaches, the sea wall, the causeways, the floods, inland to the villages and fields, twenty-seven miles across the neck of the Peninsula, Carentan to

Above: Landing craft hit on the run in. *Right:* The beach fills up as the waves flood ashore. *Below:* Waiting for the ramp to go down

There were no dry landings . . . weighed down by equipment, dragged ashore by their friends . . .

Lessay. north to Cherbourg.

H hour on the Western flank at half-past six o'clock. Tidal-variations decreed four different H hours from right to left, from 'Utah' beach to 'Sword', a span of one hour and twenty-five minutes. But the men on the right were enwrapped in their own cocoons of loneliness, in their own personal ordeals, in the pits of their stomachs, in their deaths before death, and their nine lives, transcending sea-sickness, and seventy hours in the enclosed hulls of ships. Now, in the bitter morning, they were buffeted in the shallow draft vessels, the dark sky above them wild with the roar of aircraft, the crescendo rising, the blasting roar of the main armament, the scream of shells, and all around a turbulence of men and craft.

To the left, for nearly fifty miles, variations on the theme were unfolding over the waters, 'Omaha', 'Gold', 'Juno', 'Sword', and over the dark shore-line from end to end the dust was rising, blasted in towering columns by shells and bombs to hang an opaque and ominous curtain, above the stage.

Meanwhile the struggle on the water was for the boat crews, manoeuvring their shallow draft vessels. The men in the leading assault craft knew nothing of the fate of their control vessels, one of which had fouled an obstacle, another sunk. One of the tank landing craft carrying four DD swimming tanks, to go in with the assault, blew up and sank, and then there were seven tank landing craft, twenty-eight tanks instead of thirty-two.

Enemy air bursts over the water, the spasmodic explosions of mines, the shouts of men floundering, arms flung out, weighed down by equipment, the last unheard cries of the lost, the total personal tragedies, no louder than the plaintive squeaking of mice in an uproar of lions, provided the orchestration of war. Sixty men of Battery B, 29th Field Artillery Battalion, had become a statistic on the debit side, dark shadows threshing in the turmoil, on the water, under

Ships slewed in the sand runnels . . . men flung ashore

Desperately, they dug in to hold what little had been won

the water, a piece of the pattern at the bottom of the sea.

But the pattern advanced, untroubled by calamity, the second wave, the bulldozers on their craft, the special engineer units, all in position, while the heavy armament of the bombarding squadron blasted the grey dawn to crimson shreds,

103

forty minutes to go. 276 aircraft of the US 9th Air Force roared in over the beach defences, delivering their bombs, 4,404 bombs each of 250 pounds upon seven targets, 'according to the book'.

Seventeen of the thirty-three supporting craft seemed to tear the crackling scalp off the universe in an

Still the men flooded ashore, adding to the chaos on the beach

unbearable rasping agony as their mattresses of rockets shuddered inshore, the others machine gunning, perhaps in the hope of detonating mines, perhaps simply to boost morale, but all 'drenching the beaches with

fire'.

Seven hundred yards to go, and on time, 10 assault craft, 300 men on the left, 10 assault craft, 300 men on the right. In their wakes 28 DD tanks, swimming, slopping the choppy water across their grey backs, the long muzzles of their guns like snouts, a seeming miracle thanks to the bold initiative and swift decision of their commander to launch close in at 3,000 yards, 'not according to the book.'

The beach was almost invisible behind the sand pall, blasted by gunfire and bombs, joining it to the sky, and in it, under it, the enemy – if there could be an enemy!

Sixty-seven of the bombers had

At the water's edge, the casualty list began

failed to release their bombs, one-third of the remainder had fallen between high and low water mark, the bulk of the remainder on the fortifications of La Madeleine.

Out of the leading wave of assault craft smoke projectiles hurtled to the sky, demanding silence from the gunners of the bombarding force. Three hundred yards to go, heads up, bodies tensed, the breath of life held and the ramps are down, three hundred men of the 2nd Battalion, waist deep in water, floundering, finding their feet, wading in, rifles held high, to the dry sand, and the sudden upsurge of spirit, the exultant yell of birth.

Normandy, the first men ashore, and not a shot out of the haze of battle, the grey shapes of the tanks crawling up out of the deep in their 'skirts', striking terror to the few who still lifted up their heads in the defences and dared to fire, a few wavering shots, 'desultory fire'.

These few men, and their comrades landing within minutes on their right,

did not know that they were more than a mile south of their target, that the south-easterly set of the tide, and the loss of their control craft, had brought them astride Exit 2, instead of the more heavily defended Exit 3.

Two hours later the leading troops were off the beach. The enemy strong points yielded to mopping-up operations in company strength, and the sea wall did not demand assault. Long before noon the 1st Battalion cleaned up the La Madeleine position, and opened the exit three causeway on the road to Audoville-la-Hubert, while the 2nd and 3rd Battalions crossed the causeways to Pouppeville and Houdienville, flanked by their DD tanks wading the floods, and shooting them through.

Behind them the engineers, abandoning their original plan to clear six lanes, opened up the beach without getting their feet wet, while the bulldozers heaved the masses of angle iron out of the road, and engineer detachments blasted ways through the sea wall.

Six battalions of infantry had begun to move off the beach by ten

Isolated groups made their way towards the perimeter

o'clock, and little more than an occasional air burst hampered the engineers at their toil, or reminded them of their extreme vulnerability as they placed their charges by hand. By noon the beach had been cleared at a cost of six men killed and thirty-nine wounded out of the four hundred involved in static rôles, all of them sitting ducks without cover, and without armour.

Shortly after middle-day three battalions of the 22nd Infantry Regiment were moving north to open the northerly exit, the 3rd Battalion along the coast road to anchor a flank on Hamel-de-Cruttes, the 1st and 2nd Battalions wading diagonally, and miserably, waist deep, but often armpit and neck deep, across the floods almost all the way to St. Germain de Varreville.

The 12th Infantry Regiment found the going even worse, for impatient of waiting for the 1st Battalion of the 8th Regiment to clear the causeway of exit three, they struck out wading from the Grand Dune position immediately backing the beach, crossing the line of march as they reached dry land, many of them wet to the ears.

In all that day, the 8th and 22nd Infantry Regiments lost twelve men killed. Twenty times the number would have been counted fortunate; one hundred times it a misfortune to be looked for. A single resolute man armed with a flint lock could have accounted for more than twelve men on the beach in the first half an hour, including a Brigadier-General and a Colonel.

The struggle of the 4th Infantry Division was mainly against the forces of nature, which were considerable. Eastwards it was different.

The beach of 'Omaha' lies between the outcropping rocks of Pointe de la Percée in the west, and Port-en-Bessin in the east, a shallow arc of sand enclosed inland by bluffs rising in a gentle slope one hundred and fifty feet to a plateau of tiny hedge enclosed fields, deep lanes and scattered hamlets built solidly of stone. It is a thinly populated region, the largest village, Trévières, three or four miles inland

Dazed and bewildered, the wounded, the lost and the badly frightened huddle in what shelter they can find

on the south side of the river Aure, counting not more than eight hundred inhabitants.

Three coastal villages, Vierville, St. Laurent and Colleville lie behind the beach at regular intervals a mile and a half apart, and linked by a narrow lane, from five hundred to a thousands yards in from the shore line. A stretch of paved promenade along the 'front', and with a score or more of good houses between Vierville and St. Laurent, backs a low sea wall of masonry and wood. Narrow gullies opening from the beach give access up narrow lanes to the villages.

At low tide the sands slope gradually to the sea wall, and in places to a heavy shingle bank of stones three inches in diameter, a barrier eight to ten feet high between the beach and the reedy grasses of the bluffs. Seaward the stresses of the sea and the strong currents carve runnels in the wet ribbed sands.

The rocky shoulders of the bluffs of 'Omaha', flanking the crescent of the beach, provided concealed gun

positions to enfilade the fore shore and the sea approaches, and behind the obstacle of the heavy shingle bank and the wall, the enemy wire defended entrenchments linking strong points, pillboxes, and concrete gun emplacements sited to bring devastating crossfire to bear upon the beach. Theoretically, at least, light and heavy machine guns, anti-tank guns, 75- and 88-mm. artillery pieces, would make a beaten zone of the entire beach area from end to end. And behind the forward defensive positions the terraced slopes of the bluffs gave cover to further trench systems, machine gun nests, and minefields.

The beach itself was moderately mined, especially in the areas between the gullies, and from low to high water mark an elaborate system of staggered lethal obstacles, seemed to defy the passage of any craft larger than a matchbox. But all these things had been studied in some detail by small parties visiting the beaches by night, and from countless air photographs.

'Omaha' beach held no mystery and no surprises. Even the bringing in of a new and vastly superior division – the 352nd – had been observed by British Intelligence, and passed on to US 1st Army. Unhappily, this piece of information had seemed suspect to the 1st Army Command, and the assault troops were not informed. Yet it is inconceivable that they had been briefed to expect less than the worst the enemy could be expected to perform.

General Bradley's plan was for his troops to assault head-on against the strongest points, while his highly trained engineer teams, humping their heavy equipment by hand, and in the open, cleared lanes through the obstacles and mine-fields for the follow-up troops, armour and artillery. Still on their feet, and fully exposed, they would then blow gaps in the shingle bank and sea wall.

Assaulting with the 116th and 16th Regimental Combat teams and supporting armour and artillery, Bradley planned to drive through the villages of Vierville, St. Laurent and Colleville to bestride the Isigny-Bayeux road by nightfall, embracing Trévières across the river Aure, to lie with his right on the line of the Aure floods, and his left on the western ridge of the valley of the Drôme, the boundary of the 1st US and 2nd British Armies.

At H hour US Rangers would assault a powerful enemy battery position on the sheer cliffs of the Pointe du Hoe, west of 'Omaha' beach, and eliminate a threat to both east and west. The Rangers would then form the westernmost prong of the sweep towards Isigny, with the 1st Battalion of the 116th Regiment on their left.

Such was the 'D day' intention of the V Corps.

Rangers scale the cliff gully

At three o'clock on the morning of the 6th June, Force O, commanded by Rear Admiral Hall, USN, and carrying 34,000 men and 3,300 vehicles and with a follow-up force, almost its equal, a few hours astern, began to put its assault craft into the water twelve miles off shore. There followed four hours of a macabre Dantesque confusion, through which men struggled blindly with the sea, knowing the dregs of misery, and a prey to despair. While the larger vessels moved forward, finding difficulty in maintaining their stations in the heavy sea, the smaller craft were exposed to the full force of the north westerly, fighting seas up to six feet high, unstable and making water too fast for the pumps.

Some of the larger ships had put their assault craft into the water fully loaded, but others had put their men over the side into craft pitching and rolling wildly, an ordeal for men wracked with sea-sickness. The sea, unfriendly through all the hours of the long passage, became in minutes a dark heaving formless jungle upon which men and boats wrestled like the damned in a labyrinthine maze of driven spume.

Almost at once ten small craft foundered, and upwards of three hundred men struggled for their lives in a darkness which seemed to contain a kind of uproar in its relentless and impersonal violence. Rudderless, foundering small craft and the sodden wreckage of equipment added to the menace, buffeting the men in their life jackets.

In nearly two hundred assault craft, the crews and troops who must presently assault the enemy across open beaches in the face of withering fire, baled with their tin hats for their lives, in some boats one hundred per cent. sea-sick, in all boats sodden, cramped and cold.

The official record notes that the degree of sickness varied amongst those who had had the same breakfast, but this was not a case of breakfast, a meal in which men with the tension of assault already in guts wracked with sea-sickness through two days and nights had little appetite, and for whom even a smoke had lost appeal. At last, on the verge of nervous and physical exhaustion the assault troops neared the shore, and their craft strove to manoeuvre for the final run-in. Nothing lightened with the dawn except the sky, and even then a thick haze of smoke obscured the shore.

But these men in the vanguard were more naked than they knew, or greatly cared. Behind them the seas had stripped them steadily of guns and armour, and the teams of combat engineers had suffered no less than they. With a reckless irresponsibility the Commander of the Tank landing craft carrying 32 DD tanks due to land at H minus five launched his massive vehicles into the steep seas six thousand yards off shore. Even with well trained crews there would have been small hopes for the tanks; as it was twenty-seven were swamped within minutes and sank. Two, by brilliant seamanship and chance kept afloat and reached the shore. Three others were saved the ordeal by the jamming of the ramp of the landing craft, and were carried in. Thus the 96 tanks planned to provide vital close support for the 1,450 men and eight companies, and

the first wave of the engineer teams in the moment of assault had dwindled by almost a third of their number before the battle. There were to be further losses going in to land, but these would be the natural fruits of war. The commanders of the remaining LCT's chose to run the gauntlet of fire and mines rather than give their cargoes to the sea.

Disaster had also met the attempts to ferry the supporting artillery ashore in DUKWS. The small overloaded craft, almost unmanageable, quickly foundered. The 111th Field Artillery Battalion lost all its 105-mm. howitzers save one. The 16th Infantry Cannon Company shared the same fate, and the 7th Field Artillery was very little better. The engineer teams, off-loading their heavy equipment from LCT's also had their troubles and their losses. Nevertheless, in the last hour a great concourse of men, guns and armour approached the lethal regions of the shallows, their initial losses far less than must have been inflicted by an enemy capable even of a moderate challenge on the sea and in the air. But the sea and air belonged to the Allies. With forty minutes still to go the powerful bombarding squadron opened fire on the coastal defences with a great armament from the 16-inch guns of the battleships to the 5-inch guns of the destroyers, deluging the line of the bluffs with fire and smoke. At the same time 329 out of the 446 Liberators sent to do the job attacked thirteen targets on and about the beaches with more than one thousand tons of bombs.

From ten minutes to six o'clock until five minutes before H hour it was impossible for the men cramped in the narrow steel shells of the assault craft to distinguish any kind of pattern, except that most of it was obviously going one way. They were at the core of a vast uproar, enveloping them in their own essential loneliness. They knew that the rocket craft in close support were firing short, but it did not worry them. The din was insane. They did not know that the great tide of Liberators roaring overhead had failed to loose a single bomb on the beach targets, and that baffled by the haze and smoke, and fearful of hitting their own men, they

Gradually order came out of chaos

Prisoners were brought in – a mixed bag

had decanted their bombs up to three miles inland. The men leading the assault only knew that something had gone wrong when they saw the unscarred beaches.

The leading assault craft were some eight hundred yards out when the barrage behind them lifted and the vast uproar muted to the violent staccato sounds of the guns in the close support craft in their wakes. The crash of bursting mortar bombs, of shells, and the smash of machine gun bullets against the ramps, warned the assault troops that the enemy held them in his sights. Their blindness was no longer a benison. The cries of men in the water, the sudden searing sheets of flame, the thunderous explosions as craft were hit by enemy shell and mortar fire, caught them up and splintered their isolation to fragments, and the ramps went down.

There is a devastating simplicity about disaster. There were no dry landings. The assault craft, and the larger LCVP's and LCM's grounded on the sandbanks, slewed in the sand runnels, and cast scores of men knee, waist and neck deep into seas lashed not only by the wind, but by mortar bombs, shells and machine gun bullets. While isolated groups waded to the shore, dazed and bewildered by their loneliness on that five-mile-long wilderness of sand, blinded by the smoke of many fires raging on the bluffs, uncertain what to do, others, the great majority, were in the midst of infernos of exploding ammunition and engineer charges set off by direct hits. Here and there craft blew up in ferocious ovens of flame.

The LCT's of the 743rd Tank Battalion leading in the van on the right flank surged on with men diving from stricken craft on either side, seeking the shelter of the waves, while others fought for footholds, clawing their ways to the beach, weighed down with equipment, some on hands and knees, others dragging forward on their bellies, with their wounded and their wounds. But it was safer in the sea.

A direct hit on the leading LCT killed all the Company Officers save one, but eight of the D D tanks landed on the rim of the sea to open fire on the Vierville strong point; range two hundred yards. The tanks of the 743rd were getting in further east, but the men without armour had little chance. When the ramps of the leading assault craft went down the enemy machine guns tore through living flesh so that the front cavities of the vessels became in seconds raw wounds, thick with blood. Dozens leaped this way and that for their lives.

Within half-an-hour of H hour there were at least one thousand assault infantry and engineers alive on the beach and in the shallows, but they were not fighting the enemy; they were fighting quite simply for survival, many exhausted, all too weary to drag their equipment across the beach, very few amongst them able to run, to assault, head-on, the enemy strong points.

Some went back to the water, and came in with the tide until at last it brought them, like flotsam, to the meagre shelter of the sea wall or the shingle bank. Very few of those scattered, almost at random, along the length of that beach, and all trained for the specific tasks with which, it was planned, they would be faced, knew where they were. Very few had come in on those 'stages' for which they had rehearsed. Boat teams, organised as fighting units, were miserably scrambled, and often alone, a detachment here, another two, three hundred, even a thousand yards away. For all many of them knew they were alone on the beach known as 'Omaha'. The sea was behind them, and the blinding smoke, saving them from enemy fire in the lucky places, dazed them. The few officers were often slow to get their bearings, or to make up their minds what to do. Few found the leadership in that first hour which alone could have got them off the beach. Above all they were exhausted, and there was no refuge.

The engineer combat teams, coming in on the heels of the assault infantry, had suffered severely on the run-in losing much of their vital equipment. Direct hits had blown some of their craft to pieces. Of sixteen teams, each trained for its special rôle in its sector, only five came near to their assignments, and of these, three were

utterly alone, unprotected by man or gun, naked to the enemy. Within minutes only three bulldozers out of sixteen survived for the work of heaving aside the heavy barriers of angle iron and obstacles, and these lost their ability to manoeuvre as men took cover behind them.

Yet despite their crippling losses, and their exposure to the full force of enemy fire, the engineers salvaged what gear they could and strove to clear lanes through which the follow-up forces hoped to pass. Heavy mortaring and shell fire detonated chains of fuses painfully laid by hand, and blew up whole detachments of engineers before they could get clear. The swiftly rising tide foamed round their feet, their waists, submerging the outer obstacles, and forcing the survivors to the sea wall and the shingle before their tasks were a tenth-part done. On the whole sector of the 116th RCT they had cleared two gaps. Far to the east, where scarcely a man had landed, they had cleared four gaps, but of them all only one was marked. The effort had cost more than 40 per cent of the engineer strength, most of it in the first half-hour.

But always behind the engineers, not only the rising tide, but the tremendous tide of men and vehicles pressing on, steadily wave upon wave, building up on the beaches, in the shallows, demanding an outlet. After three terrible hours the foreshore was a wilderness of wreckage, of burning vehicles, of shattered craft, and shattered men. Not one of the exits was open, not one of the defensive positions had been stormed, and a message went back to the sea to land no more vehicles, but only men.

Nevertheless, long before the destroyers of the Naval Force came close inshore to blaze away at the enemy strong points at little more than a thousand yards, a desperate beginning of order was growing out of chaos, and men, tried to the limits of endurance, regained their feet, lifted up their heads, and began to fight for more than their lives.

The beach of 'Omaha' had been divided into four main sections, code named from West to East, 'Charlie', 'Dog', 'Easy', 'Fox' and each of these sections, except 'Charlie' which was confined to operations of the US Rangers, sub-divided, 'Dog-Green', 'Dog-White', 'Dog-Red', embracing the right wing from Vierville to St Laurent; 'Easy-Green', 'Easy-Red' in the centre, from the St Laurent gully to a point immediately west of the Colleville gully; 'Fox-Green', 'Fox-Red', the first astride the Colleville gully, and eastward one thousand yards to a small gully and possible exit, the main target of 'Fox-Red'.

The Regimental boundary between the 116th RCT, and the 16th RCT lay along the dividing line of 'Easy-Green' and 'Easy-Red', but the rigours of the run-in, coupled with the strong easterly set of the current tended to drag the whole assault eastward and distort the pattern out of recognition. One section of the 116th landing with a scramble of the 16th on the extreme eastern end of 'Easy-Red' was more than a thousand yards from its nearest flanking unit on 'Easy-Green'. Bush fires burning furiously on the bluffs following the naval bombardment gave isolated sections quiet landings, but left them stranded and bewildered. Officers were slow to make up their minds, and decide on action. Few could hope to carry out the specific tasks for which they had trained so arduously.

While on the flanks at 'Dog-Green' and 'Fox-Green' Companies fought for their lives four thousand yards apart, the whole central sector slowly began to stir. Leaders arose from the ranks and roused their fellows. A palsied fear of mines afflicted many throughout the whole day. A false step often meant death or the loss of limbs, and wounded men lay where they had fallen not daring to move. A whole Company moved off the beach on the left flank in single file, not daring to clear the minefield, and exposing itself for hours.

The day belonged to the few, to the lieutenant and a wounded engineer sergeant who walked erect, cut wire, and blew mines, taunting those who lay at the water's edge more by their examples than with words, until at last the scattered remnants on 'Easy-Red' staggered forward; to an engineer lieutenant crawling through mud and sand, probing for mines with a hunting knife; to the infantry lieutenant who assaulted a strong point single handed with grenades, and handed over his map and compass to a sergeant as he died, riddled with bullets. They were there, such men, in ones and twos, all along the line of smoke and mines, chaos, exhaustion and death, gathering their small groups, taunting, cursing, urging, moving forward off the beach, usually blind, but the daylight would come. Presently the fog of war would clear, and these men would combine to new tasks.

But on 'Dog-Green' and 'Fox-Green', where the leading companies had been blown to pieces, literally at the cannon's mouth, as their craft had come in against the powerful defences

of the Vierville and Colleville gullies, the pattern had a different form. On the left at 'Fox-Green' sections of the 16th and 116th came in late, scrambled together, and with their supporting DD tanks at the bottom of the sea. Deprived of almost their entire Officer and NCO leadership, battered three-quarters to death, these remnants were beyond rallying. In taking the first shock these men had played such parts as they were to play that day, and the wreckage of their dead, the sodden corpses floundering in the rising tide in all the ugly maze of lost equipment, bore witness.

The struggle belonged to those following in their wakes.

On the extreme right flank of 'Charlie', three miles west of Vierville, a special force of the 2nd Ranger Battalion, had assaulted the battery position on the Pointe du Hoe, shooting their grappling irons up and over the cliff top, and swarming up by ladders and ropes to find the position abandoned. This group then moved inland, later to draw the few available enemy reserves to counter-attack. But they had landed east of their target, and the Company of Rangers standing offshore on the right flank of 'Dog-Green', failing to receive an agreed success signal on time, went in to land through the shambles of the leading Company of the 116th Infantry against the Vierville gully. Mortared and machine gunned, and hit by anti-tank gun fire as the ramps went down, a third of their number lost, the remainder touched down and struggled doggedly over the 200 yards of open ground to the wall. Not a man had the strength to run, and many stumbled, but all had the strength of will to press on while life was in them. Sixty-two men out of one-hundred-and-thirty reached the wall.

But on the left the 5th Ranger Battalion came in behind a Company of the 116th Infantry on the 'peace' of 'Dog-White', clear between the heavily defended gullies of Vierville and St Laurent. Four-hundred-and-fifty strong the first wave reached the sea wall losing 'only five or six men', and there to join the company of the 116th.

The final spur was provided by the arrival of Brigadier-General Cota and Colonel Canham, both men fearless under fire, Cota blown off his feet by blast, Canham wounded in the wrist, but both men tirelessly organising and urging men up and over the bluffs to swing right upon Vierville. Thus a way was beginning to open on the right. Two groups each twenty strong had already reached Vierville, and the reinforcements were in time to beat off an enemy counter-attack.

On the left, in all the area of the 16th RCT of the 1st Division, a miracle, it seemed, would be needed to set the battered remnants of exhausted men on their feet. Colonel Taylor was the miracle. Bold, erect, with the natural carriage of the brave, he strode amongst the inert, disillusioned men, lacking even the strength to drag their equipment, and led them off the beaches, not as a rabble, but as men to battle for the Colleville – St Laurent exits. Two kinds of men were on the beach, he told the bodies on the wet sand, 'the dead and those who are going to die'.

But from the sea the milling craft off shore, many not daring to go in to land, looked to Colonel Talley, the Corps Commander's Special Observer, like 'a stampeded herd of cattle'. Only 100 tons out of the 2,400 tons of essential supplies needed on 'D day' went ashore. But at last men, re-inforced by the waves of the follow-up battalions, were moving off the beaches. It did not look very hopeful to the Generals in the Command Ships but the hard outer crust had broken, and the enemy was without reserves. By nightfall the Germans had lost the battle of 'Omaha' beach, but the Americans did not know that they had won it. Very few knew why and the dead would never know.

On the Eastern flank the British fought their different battle.

The debris of a dreadful day

The airborne: the eastern flank

The task of the British 6th Airborne Division was to establish a bridge-head across the river Orne and the Caen Canal, midway between the city of Caen and the Normandy coast, and to protect the Eastern flank of the Seaborne landings. They were to hold until such time as a firm lodgement area had been established.

In its initial stages the task was both complex and of a desperate simplicity; complex because the pieces in the pattern were many; simple because there was no room for finesse, no time. A number of *coups de main* must succeed, and become a simple *tour de force*. There could not be a second chance, no hope for delay in enemy reaction. Two Parachute Brigades would land in the very midst of the enemy, on the boundary of the German 7th and 15th Armies, seize the vital objectives, and at all costs prevent reinforcements from reaching the main battlefields.

Powerful elements of the German 711th and 716th Divisions defended every village, strong point and bridge; the 21st Panzer Division poised and ready to strike was on their right flank, and behind them the whole weight of the German Armoured Reserve within striking distance. Unless, therefore, the two leading Brigades of Parachute troops could strike their blows like lightning out of the sky, and consolidate, unless they could clear landing

Gliders of the 6th Airborne Division over the Channel

places for the glider-borne brigade, and could have with them anti-tank guns, mortars and the bulk of their heavy equipment, their task would be beyond hope. Whatever might be won by lightning strokes must inevitably be lost, even before the sun was up, and assuredly before the sun was down.

The 5th Parachute Brigade would seize the bridges across the Orne and the Caen Canal north of Ranville, clear and protect landing zones for their gliders, and establish a firm bridgehead.

The 3rd Parachute Brigade would demolish the bridges across the flooded river Dives at Troarn, Bures, Robehomme and Varaville. They would block and hold all routes leading in from the south east. They would destroy the powerful Merville Battery of 155-mm guns and its Garrison before it could enfilade the left flank of the Seaborne attack with devastating fire. For this latter task there would be a maximum time of one hour.

It was three-minutes-past eleven o'clock on the night of the 5th when the first of six Albemarle Aircraft of the Pathfinder Force took off from their English field with sixty men who must light the beacons to lead the way. At the same hour, six gliders bore a small force of the 2nd Battalion, the Oxford and Bucks LI and Royal Engineers to seize the crossings of the Caen Canal and the Orne. It was a

night of drizzling rain and gusty winds, and lit by tattered patches of moonlight; a night filled with the roar of aircraft, the bombers, the transports, the tugs and their gliders in their thousands teeming through the Channel sky from le Havre to Cherbourg. Below them the wakes of five thousand ships cleaving the gunmetal sea into greenish-white trails of foam.

Twenty minutes after midnight the first Pathfinders touched down on the soil of France, two-thirds blown away by the winds, beacons lost, equipment damaged, but enough on their targets to do the vital minimum as best they might. Within minutes the leading glider of the first of the *coup de main* parties crash-landed forty-seven yards from its objective, overwhelmed the enemy with the sleep still in their eyes, and seized intact the bridges over the Caen Canal and the Orne. Already the enemy tracer looped the sky, and the flak streaming up into the cloud-banks exacted a price in gliders and transports over the coast, and with small-arms fire met the men of the 7th, 12th and 13th Battalions of the 5th Brigade tumbling out of the cloud-banks. Ten seconds from sky to earth, time enough to die, to hurl grenades upon the enemy sniping the dark pendulums of the parachutes like flocks of birds. While many landed fighting, at once at grips with the enemy, others hung suspended in the trees, sitting ducks, few to survive, and difficult to rescue.

By half-past two o'clock the 7th Battalion was engaged desperately on both banks of the Orne against units of the German 716th Division and two Battalions of Feuchtinger's 21st Panzer Division, committed soon after one o'clock. One company of the 7th, hard pressed on three sides at Bénouville, absorbed a small battalion reserve of mortar men and machine gunners, unable to make contact with their weapons, and arming themselves from the captured and the dead. It was a fight against time. Relief could not reach them until early afternoon, but the colossal detonations of the naval bombardment preceding the seaborne landings, brought new inspiration.

The 12th Battalion, having seized le bas de Ranville with exemplary speed, found itself in need of luck as well as inspiration. Its forward platoons, outnumbered twenty to one, faced 88-mm guns firing point blank at seventy yards, and with the breech block of their solitary six-pounder smashed on landing, their only hope lay in the uncertainty of the enemy, and fortunately this was great. While Blumentritt strove to arouse an adequate sense of urgency in the German High Command, and obtain the release of the Armoured reserve, Speidel was advising Rommel of the situation with equal urgency, and receiving orders for the employment of the 21st Panzer Division. But Feuchtinger had committed a battle group of the 21st Panzer Division on his own initiative soon after six o'clock. Had this battle group pressed its attack it must have overwhelmed the defenders of le bas de Ranville, and gravely restricted the bridgehead. As it was, the confusion in the enemy command and the widespread threats

developing over the entire Normandy coast, was the luck the paratroops needed. At about mid-morning the German armour turned its back upon le bas de Ranville leaving the battered defenders in possession.

The effects of the struggle in the early hours on the extreme left flank, were to have a vital significance in the crises developing on 'Omaha' beach, for when Feuchtinger was ordered to move his infantry battalions to counter-attack the Americans, he was unable to extricate them from their fight with the 5th Parachute Brigade. His anti-tank battalion was also deeply committed in an attempt to save the 716th Infantry Division from destruction by the Seaborne Infantry and armour. Thus no reserves were available to move against 'Omaha' at the vital hour.

In the hours before the dawn the enemy could form no clear idea of the forces coming against him out of the sky from end to end of the Cherbourg Peninsula. He was inclined to overestimate Allied available power, and could not free his thinking from his fears for the Pas de Calais.

Meanwhile the 3rd Battalion of the 5th Parachute Brigade, the 13th, had landed well in a tight perimeter, and a strong force had advanced upon Ranville, leaving one company to clear stakes and mines against the coming of the glider-borne reinforcements. The Company knocked out three tanks with its PIAT's, but was desperately in need of anti-tank guns and heavy equipment. A Company of the 711th Infantry Division had been destroyed in Ranville, and the village and Chateau of the aged Comtesse de Rohan were in British hands by half-past two o'clock.

The 5th Parachute Brigade had assembled swiftly in sufficient force to gain its objectives, but it remained very thin on the ground, too many of its men lost in the trees, and many more engaged in a score of local savage encounters, which, in the end could and did strengthen the general position.

When the first Commandos fought their way through from the beach at Ouistreham, reaching the Orne bridgehead only two-and-a-half minutes behind schedule, the small force of

Left: Dropping zone north of Caen.
Above: Lancasters bomb German troop
concentrations north of Caen.
Below: When daylight came, the
Germans searched the skies for more
paratroops

the Oxford and Bucks Light Infantry, with the help of the 7th Battalion, had held for twelve hours against powerful counter-attacks supported by artillery and mortars. One Company, with all its officers killed or wounded, held on without relief for seventeen hours.

It was exactly two o'clock when No. 6 Commando led the way across the Orne bridge, on its way to reinforce the 9th Battalion of the 3rd Parachute Brigade. The Commando had then fought its way through enemy strong points, destroyed a battery in full blast against the beaches, and marched nine miles.

It seemed impossible – and it still does – that a coherent pattern could emerge from the complex missions of the 3rd Parachute Brigade, or that the seven major tasks, covering a seven-mile front from the town of Troarn, due east of Caen, to the coast at Merville, could be successfully fulfilled. Each demanded daring of a high order, meticulous planning, impeccable timing, and above all the ability to improvise, if, as was almost certain, things went wrong.

The Albemarles carrying advance parties with the urgent rôle of clearing a way for a small glider-borne force with anti-tank guns, dropped their cargoes reasonably near their objective, but the Brigadier, wounded and wallowing in the flooded Dives with his Headquarters, and elements of the 1st and 9th Battalions, had to take what comfort he could from his own warning words before take-off: 'Do not be daunted if chaos reigns', he had said. It was dusk when, weary and wounded, he and those with him, having suffered under the bombing of our own aircraft, struggled back to the main body of the Brigade.

The 3rd Brigade had a bad drop. The smoke and dust from the heavy bombing of the Merville Battery position obscured dropping zones on which many beacons were damaged, and failed to show up. Flak and the strong wind gusts played their parts; gliders parted from their tugs, many were hit, but above all, perhaps, 46 Group in particular had lacked the time for training. Now, on the day, on sea and land, the miserable and bitter battles waged by the 'Overlord' plan-

ners for air and sea landing craft, always denied until the last moment, were reaping a harvest in lives from end to end of the Peninsula.

The 1st (Canadian) Battalion, its primary mission to destroy the bridges at Varaville and Robehomme, was widely scattered. The 8th Battalion, headed for the Troarn and Bures bridges, then to withdraw and hold in the Bavent woods, was a little better. Both Battalions assembled a basic minimum of men and explosives, and without waiting for more, moved swiftly upon their objectives. Both Battalions had confidence that the day would add to, rather than diminish, their numbers, and in this they were wholly justified. All over that countryside, filled with friends as well as enemies, men in twos and threes homed on their units, not only running gauntlets of enemy fire, and eluding patrols, but withstanding the even more potent menace of embraces, cognac and strawberries thrust upon many of them by people wild with excitement, and releasing the pent-up emotions stored through the harsh and bitter years.

Soon after landing, the wounded Colonel of the 8th Battalion assembled 180 men, and enough explosive for the jobs, and dividing his force into two groups, advanced upon Bures and Troarn. The main force of Royal Engineers with most of the demolition equipment, had dropped too far from the target to reach the assembly area in time, but a detachment of Royal Engineers, finding themselves on the northern rim of the Bavent woods, and in possession of several hand trolleys and a jeep, foraged for explosives in the gear dropped round them, and embarked upon twin dashes for the bridges.

The trolley party, bound for the Bures bridge, quickly fell in with the advance guard of the first battalion group, and performed their task covered by paratroops more or less in the manner intended, but the Troarn party meanwhile were in the midst of a wild adventure vouchsafed to the few, and blessed by the gods. A major and seven men took the road to Troarn in the jeep, a sapper armed with

The end of a long night

a Bren acting as 'rear-gunner', while the others used their Stens. A 'knife-rest' barbed barrier blocked the way to the level-crossing in front of the town, and by the time they had cut their way through, the whole garrison was aroused. Undaunted, and almost certainly in their hour of exaltation unaware that they were even vulnerable, they tore through the main street of Troarn, blazing away like an exploding firework, and on down the steep hill to the valley bridge pursued by machine gun bullets clipping the trees just above their heads.

It took the small party five minutes to blow a gap twenty feet wide out of the bridge, ditch the jeep, and disappear into the darkness. It is improbable that the thought of failure occurred to any one of them. All reached the Brigade rendezvous at le Mesnil, and at dusk the 8th Battalion, grown to 230 strong, took up its holding position in the Bavent woods.

On the left the Canadians of the 1st Battalion, short of men after their bad drop, found sufficient strength to press home immediate attacks on their objectives at Varaville and Robehomme. While all kinds and conditions of French men, women and children, helped stragglers to rejoin their battalion, the solid nucleus of one company attacked Varaville, destroyed the bridge, and at once became too heavily engaged to extricate itself until late in the morning. Meanwhile, a Captain of Royal Engineers with elements of the Battalion, blew the Robehomme bridge.

But these exploits, performed with satisfactory speed in spite of the chaos predicted by the Brigadier, were outshone that morning by a deed of a different order. This was the assault on the Merville Battery position.

The 150-mm guns of Merville were housed in concrete emplacements six feet six inches thick, reinforced by twelve feet of earthworks, and protected by steel doors. The perimeter fence, lined with a concertina barbed wire barrier fifteen feet wide and five feet high, enclosed an area of some 400 square yards defended by a garrison of 130 men. At least twenty weapon pits and machine gun positions were sited to protect every possible avenue of approach through surrounding mine-fields, and with no cover from fire available to attackers in the open fields and orchards. At least one 20-mm dual-purpose gun completed the known armament of a battery which threatened the left flank of the sea-borne attack at close range, and was capable of creating havoc on the sea-borne approaches. It was imperative that its guns should be destroyed. Direct hits by heavy bombs had failed to penetrate the casemates, and the naval gunfire to be directed against the battery if all else failed could only hope to put the guns out of action by direct hits through the embrasures or up the 'spouts'. Such hits occur by mere chance, and are not to be looked for.

A force of one hundred Lancasters unloading a deluge of 4,000-pound bombs shortly after midnight failed to hit the target, but killed a number of cattle and provided some deep craters which might be useful cover for the attackers.

In the last four or five minutes of the flight from England, enemy flak forced pilots to take evasive action, and tumbled the battalion commander into the garden of a German head-quarters. The rest of the force lay scattered over an area ten times as large as it should have been. Yet, at ten-minutes-to-three o'clock in the morning the Colonel, having found his own feet, had assembled 150 men, one Vickers heavy machine gun, a bare minimum of signals equipment, and twenty lengths of bangalore torpedo. Jeeps, six-pounders, mortars, sappers, mine detectors, had all gone astray. With this force, organised in companies some 30 strong, and in small groups with special missions, the Colonel proposed to attack.

Fortunately, the small reconnais-sance party had dropped well, established a firm base according to plan, cut through the outer perimeter fence, and crouched close up against the enemy wire trying to detect the exact positions of enemy posts from the snatches of talk they were able to overhear. A second party had cut three paths through the minefields, and laid tapes.

The attack upon the battery had been meticulously planned, and exhaustively rehearsed. Every man of the 8th Parachute Battalion, and the small force of volunteers with the 591st Parachute Squadron, Royal Engineers, whose object was to crash-land in three gliders on top of the enemy guns, had studied every inch of the ground from air photographs and large scale models. There would be very little margin for error.

Up to a few minutes before the arrival of two gliders overhead the enemy had given no sign of being alert to an impending attack, yet ten machine guns, six of them outside the perimeter fence, immediately blazed into action against the 150 men of the Battalion as they reached the firm base position. It was then just on half-past four o'clock.

It was immediately evident that the glider-crash party would fail. One glider had parted from its tow rope on the way, and the two remaining, one of which had had a rough passage, were laced with anti-aircraft fire from the 20-mm guns of the battery. Both glider pilots had found it difficult to disentangle the exact position from the wilderness of the Dives floods, and one had mistaken the village of Merville for the Battery. At the same time the men on the gound had been unable to fire the promised star-shells to guide them in. One glider landed four miles from the target, its crew joining up with the Brigade at le Mesnil, while the other, narrowly avoiding a minefield, crash-landed in flames within two hundred yards of the firm base.

For four desperate hours, the crew, wounded and whole, tumbling from the burning glider, held off an attack from a platoon of enemy, and success-fully prevented reinforcements from reaching the battery.

At that moment, within a minute or two of half-past four o'clock, the as-sault went in. Three small breaching parties blew gaps in the wire, and the assault parties, following the tapes through the minefield, the bomb craters and the tangles of wire, closed with the enemy. While the main assault went in from the south-east a sergeant and six men, skilfully build-ing up a pattern of fire, put in a feint attack against the main north gate.

Half-an-hour later, after a hand to hand melée of a desperate and deadly intensity, the success signal blazed out. It had been a fight of gaunt shadow shapes against a spasmodic background of smoke, flame and explosion. One of the battery guns had been destroyed by firing two shells simultaneously, and the other three by gammon bombs. A lieutenant, dying of his wounds, checked the destruction and was added to the sixty-six British dead. Thirty more men were wounded, twenty seriously. Not a man of the party was over twenty-one years of age. Few had fought before.

By early evening the two Brigades of the British Sixth Airborne Division, anxiously awaiting their glider and seaborne reinforcements, had carried out their tasks, and established a bridgehead across the Caen Canal and the Orne. They had been strengthened by the arrival of the 1st Commando Brigade, and had blocked all roads from the east. Their future – if they were to have a future – must depend on the success or failure of the 3rd British Infantry Division, spearhead-ing the left flank assault on the beaches.

By evening it had become clear that the advance out of the beachhead was too slow. Infantry had dug in too soon, when they should have pressed on. Traffic jams building up on the beach prevented the British from shaking loose until early afternoon, and Feuchtinger's armour, at last with its orders, was driving down, nearly ninety tanks strong, to the sea at Lion sur Mer. Nevertheless, the diver-sion of the German armour to meet the major threat of the British land-ing, had saved the airborne from being overwhelmed.

Left, right, and centre

The battle for the Orne bridgehead was already six hours old when Hobart's armour led the British and Canadian seaborne assaults to the rock enclosed strips of beach fronting Ouistreham and Lion sur Mer, Langrune and Courselles, la Riviére and le Hamel. Far away on the right, beyond the out-cropping rocks of Port-en-Bessin, the Americans had suffered for a full hour under the guns of the enemy strong points on the long bare stretch of 'Omaha'. The hopes of surprise in the east had seeped away, but it appeared to make no difference in an enemy hammered from the sea and sky.

A smoke screen veiled the whole British left flank from the powerful guns of the le Havre batteries, which had withstood a hundred batterings from the air, and were a graver menace than the rough sea to the great convoys assembling seven-and-a-half miles off shore, and putting their hordes of small craft into the water. Enemy E boats, choosing their moment to venture out of le Havre, emerged momentarily from the smoke to discharge four torpedoes, one to sink a Norwegian destroyer, another to force the Command ship, HMS Largs, full astern in evasive action, the remaining two to pass harmlessly between the warships.

15-inch guns of H.M.S. Warspite pound the eastern beaches

British bombardment of the mouth of the Orne, seen from the German positions

Yet the hour, trained for, planned for, dreamed about since Dunkirk, and which was at last about to strike, seemed in a manner unreal, and strangely calm. Many at sea felt a sense of anti-climax, and experiences in the assault craft were of a variety to make one feel that here were a hundred battles bewilderingly diverse. The hell and horror of one man was a 'piece of cake', in the jargon of the day, to another one hundred feet or yards away. A battle is always the totality of its parts.

A helmsman was seen to be hanging out behind his assault craft acting as a human rudder, steering it in. Men floundered here and there to death by drowning, the assault and landing craft surged on seeming borne on the screaming, crashing ferocity of their own gun craft, blazing away with 4.7's, rockets, oerlikons and machine guns, while the armour and field artillery went into action from their carrying craft. Mines, mortar bombs, and shells erupted small craft out of the water to fill air and sea with falling wreckage, explosions seemed to tear the entrails out of larger vessels, and to leap into furnaces in which, miraculously, men survived.

The high wind was piling the rising tide above the outer belts of obstacles, and there was nothing for it but to ride in, attempting to navigate the lethal forest of angle iron, stakes and steel, and crash down in the foam of waves breaking on the shore. Every man knew from maps and models the lay-out of narrow streets behind the sea walls, the narrow channels leading through to the objectives, la Riva Farm, Hermanville, the Périers Ridge, the road to Caen. But all that seemed infinitely remote, things for other men, even in another life, to think on. The minds of the troops of the British 3rd Infantry Division, coming in to land on the two sectors of 'Sword' beach code named, 'Queen Red' and 'Queen White', were absorbed by the beach, the immediate strip to be conquered, the mines, the machine guns and 88's sited to make a beaten zone of every yard of the way. After

that – if there was an after to that – would be another story.

H hour was half-past seven o'clock, with the armour leading in at H minus five. Force S for 'Sword' had put its DD tanks into the water three miles out, and it was clear that only magnificent seamanship on the part of their crews, the 13/18th Hussars, would bring them in on time, or at all. Low in the water, beaten by waves four feet high, the grey upper works were almost invisible, and a line of Tank landing craft cutting across their bows sank two, and might have swamped a score but for a mattress of rockets falling short, and forcing the Tank landing craft to alter course.

When the bombardment of the warships began to lift, the shore approaches were a turmoil of weaving craft and wreckage, and almost to the minute the flail tanks crawled on shore in the lead, eight assault teams, beating up towards the exits, engaging enemy guns point blank, followed by the whole strange galaxy of armoured monsters, the bridging tanks, the bobbins, the petards, and thirty-three out of forty DD tanks crawling up

out of the water in time to shoot the infantry over the hazardous stretch of beach.

Within minutes the wreckage of armour added a grotesque dimension to the inferno. A flail, losing its tracks, continued to engage an enemy 88, another brewed, a bridging tank lost its bridge, and somewhere a DD tank foundered in a bewildering mass of steel. Sappers leaving their armoured vehicles pressed on, clearing by hand.

The Germans watch and wait

133

First wave Commandos go in, the special tanks of 79th Armoured Div clearing the way

The special tanks clearing the beaches

Commandos wait to go in

Like prehistoric monsters, the Flails and Crocodiles go in

View from the beach

13th/18th Hussars ashore at last

Canadian troops pour ashore

Silhouettes of war

Men leapt from blazing craft in the shallows, and struggled towards the beach through the crumpled ruins of men and equipment. On the right, the 1st Battalion of the South Lancashire Regiment, spearheading the 8th Infantry Brigade, quickly cleared the beach in the wake of the armour, and began to assault the strong points. The 2nd

Royal Marines clear of the beach at St Aubin sur Mer

Battalion, the East Yorkshire Regiment, their brothers-in-arms on the left, fought their way more slowly to a foothold. Over all the beach, left and right, enemy mortar and small-arms fire was intense, thickened by the anti-tank guns on Périers Ridge, and the divisional artillery ranging on the barrage balloons.

Out of the seeming chaos and confusion, and the increasing wreckage on the beach, the threads of order began to emerge. By half-past nine o'clock Hobart's armour, manned by the 22nd Dragoons, the Westminster Dragoons and two Squadrons of the 5th Assault Regiment, Royal Engineers, had cleared seven out of eight lanes through the exits. At la Riva Farm, the Squadrons were rallying, some to aid Commando troops fighting for possession of the Ouistreham Locks, and for Lion-sur-Mer, others making ready to spearhead the infantry on the road to Caen.

The South Lancashires reached Hermanville in good time, one-and-a-half miles inland, confronting the vital Périers Ridge, bristling with Feuchtinger's anti-tank guns and defended by Infantry of the 716th Division. But the 8th Infantry Brigade had lost its vital momentum. Enemy guns broke up armoured sorties, and the infantry dug in at Hermanville. The men had fixed their eyes and their imaginations upon the beaches for too long a time, and in that hour of achievement the mechanism of nervous exhaustion demanded a pause. Meanwhile, by eleven o'clock, the 185th Brigade was assembling its three battalions in the orchards beyond Hermanville, and an immediate attack should have been pressed home against the Périers Ridge, not only to open the road to Caen, but for the urgent relief of the Orne bridgehead. Where commando troops had marched boldly through the infantry, dourly led, performed its slow set-piece gyrations.

A contributory cause of the slowness in front was, however, the growing mass of men and armour, striving to break loose from the beaches, and the impossible tangles of traffic in the narrow streets, the laterals and leads out of the exits. The tanks of the Staffordshire Yeomanry, with the rôle of carrying the men of the King's Shropshire Light Infantry on the road to Caen, could not be prized loose from the melée. It was late when the guns of the Périers Ridge were silenced, and the Shropshire s took the road alone.

The infantry of the line did all that its leaders demanded but it was not enough. The East Yorkshires had taken a severe hammering, losing five officers and sixty men killed, and more than one hundred and forty wounded, in gaining their objectives. The Shropshires on the lonely road out of Hermanville were marching boldly into the midst of the enemy, their flanks bare. One Company silenced a battery shelling the line of march at close range, and at four o'clock in the afternoon the Battalion, joined by the self-propelled guns and armour of the Staffordshire Yeomanry, reached Biéville, barely three-and-a-half miles short of Caen.

It was, in fact, a position of extreme difficulty, for at last Feuchtinger had his clear orders, Rommel was speeding on his way to his Command, Hitler had awakened from the effects of his sleeping pills, and the German armour was on the move. At Biéville twenty-four tanks leading a powerful battle group of the 21st Panzer Division, probing for a crevice in the British assault, clashed head-on with the Shropshires and their armour. Self-propelled guns accounted for five enemy tanks, and the enemy withdrew. In spite of the armoured threats the Shropshires strove to press on, only to be halted by intense fire from the thickly wooded Lebisey Ridge, and demanding a full battalion attack. Casualties were growing steadily; a renewed armoured attack might develop at any moment, and the flanking battalions of the 185th Brigade were making very slow progress. Caen was fading to a dream.

But Feuchtinger's armour was not coming that way again. The British, now in command of the Périers Ridge, had pushed the battle group further west, and the spearhead, bouncing off the Shropshires, and

again off the British guns, was pounding northward down the wide gap between the British and Canadian landings, ninety tanks strong. There was nothing to stop them.

The main weight of the British sea-borne assault fell on the right, on the beach code named 'Gold', a shallow arc streaked with treacherous strands of soft clay, and behind that to the west the powerful strong points and fortified villages of Arromanches and le Hamel, and to the east, la Rivière. A sanitorium at le Hamel, masked from naval gunfire by its peculiarly sheltered position and by immensely strong concrete fortifications on its seaward side, mounted an ominous array of weapons capable of bringing down devastating enfilade fire upon the beaches at high watermark and above. The traverse of its guns had been sacrificed in favour of impregnability seaward, and its power could not be brought to bear upon the sea approaches. It had survived many bombing attacks. Behind it lay a dangerous stretch of marsh. la Rivière, on the left flank, was no less strongly fortified and held, but it lacked outstanding features.

None doubted that a fierce and deadly welcome awaited the British 50th Division, the Northumbrian Division, as soon as its leading Brigades set foot ashore in the tracks of twelve assault teams of Hobart's armour.

The 50th Division had fought its way doggedly backwards and forwards, into and out of France, North Africa and Sicily, at Dunkirk, Gazala, Mersa Matruh, Alamein, the Mareth Line, Wadi Akarit, and Catania. There was no longer anything very much 'Northumbrian' about it, except that it had inherited and preserved something of the rugged instincts of those rugged people. As a Division it had acquired an 'esprit' usually the prerogative of Regiments, and on the morning of the 6th June, its Brigades and Battalions rode the breakers to the beaches of le Hamel and la Rivière to open the last chapter of their story.

As soon as the mind grapples with the importance of one beach above another it is evident that all are vital links in a chain which must hold. On the British Second Army Front, the importance of covering the left flank, and preventing the German armour and reinforcements reaching the Normandy battlefields, needs no emphasis. On the right, Arromanches, the site designate for the British Mulberry, must be cleared in depth with a minimum of delay, and the boundary between the British and American Armies made good by the rapid seizure of Port-en-Bessin, the rail head and port serving Bayeux. In the centre, the Canadians, faced with a most difficult landing menaced by rocks and reefs as well as a full measure of man-made obstacles, must move with all speed to give depth to the whole centre front.

East of the Canadians on 'Juno' beach, from Courselles to Lion, and west of the British right flank on 'Gold' beach, lay dangerous stretches of rocky coast, the first of which gave the name to Calvados, and which must be penetrated and cleared to link up the bridgeheads. This dangerous task was the rôle of the 41st, 47th and 48th Royal Marine Commandos.

It was twenty-five minutes past seven o'clock when the leading flotillas carrying the flail tanks and armoured fighting vehicles of the Westminster Dragoons and the 81st and 82nd Assault Squadrons, Royal Engineers, closed the beaches of le Hamel and la Rivière. It was at once clear that the heavy air and naval bombardment had failed to silence the enemy guns, especially on the right. An 88-mm gun firing from the cliff top west of le Hamel hit the leading vessel amidships, wrecked the engine room, and slewed the ship broadside on to the beach. Striving to land from this position the first of the flail tanks sank, and the whole of No. 1 team was immobilised to await the turn of the tide.

Only one of the flails serving the 231st Brigade's right flank succeeded in beating a lane up and off the beach, while in its tracks others foundered, losing their tracks to mines and heavy machine-gun fire. On-coming craft, driven like surf boats by the strong wind and heavy sea, fouled obstacles and armour, creating a sense of chaos on the edge of the sea. The Squadron Commander of the right flanking teams was killed at the outset in the turret of his AVRE, but

many armoured vehicles, temporarily unable to crawl, engaged the enemy with their main armament, and were as valuable to some as cover, as they were a hindrance to others. But further east, beyond the immediate beaten zone of fire from the le Hamel strong points, the three assault teams serving the left flank of the Brigade made good progress. While flails lashed the beach, lumbering on in the midst of eruptions of mines, mud and sand, to gain the coast road, the bobbins laid mattresses over patches of soft blue clay, and fascine and bridging tanks crawled over the beach with their huge unwieldy burdens, finally to fill the craters, to make crossable the anti-tank barriers and ditches, to pave the way for infantry, armour and the great mass of vehicles bearing down, with a pressure impossible to deny, upon the beaches.

The DD tanks, finding the sea passage to the beach hopeless under their own power in the rough conditions, had been held back, later to beach dry shod, and add greatly to the early armoured fire power. Meanwhile, the spearhead rôle belonged to the flails and their supporting AVRE's.

Well within the hour, Hobart's armour had emerged from the chaos of the water's edge and cleared four safe lanes out of six over the le Hamel beaches, and spearheaded the leading battalions of the 231st Brigade onto their objectives. Petard tanks all along the line were dealing out murderous treatment to fortified houses and strong points which would have tied up infantry platoons and companies, perhaps for hours, and taken a steady toll in dead.

On the 69th Brigade front facing la Rivière the flails and AVRE's of the assault teams fought their way with the infantry across the beaches in the face of intense mortar, anti-tank and machine-gun fire directed from well sited pillboxes, and houses linked together in systems of strong points. Three clear lanes were opened out of six from the edge of the sea to the edge of the marshland beyond the coast road. While Petard tanks supporting the infantry blasted the coastal crust of strong points with their giant mortars, like ancient cannon, AVRE's filled craters and

142

Left: The move inland. *Above:* House to house fighting begins

anti-tank ditches with fascines, provided soft landings for armour behind walls, bridged culverts, and bulldozed tracks for the host of vehicles and men coming in fast on the rising tide. Within the hour armour and infantry were more than a mile inland, and the hard outer crust of the defence was broken.

Yet so limited is the vision of men in battle that all this may seem a travesty of the truth to the 1st Battalion of the Hampshire Regiment, leading on the right flank. For them the sea-sick pills had not worked. They had had an uneasy passage, finally debouched from their assault craft thirty yards out into waves beating about their thighs and dragging their feet as they struggled to the dry sand. They had come in supported by self-propelled guns and field artillery firing from their carrying craft, aware of mortar and machine-gun fire from the enemy over the last half-mile. It had been uncomfortable rather than deadly.

Smoke and flame obscured the beaches, but it seemed that the terrific bombing, followed by the naval bombardment, had failed to silence the enemy. On the beach, in their first moments of comparative immunity before they came within the traverse of the le Hamel guns, they saw only the confusion of disabled armour, and swiftly discovered that for two-thirds of their numbers there were no safe lanes across the shambles of the beach. An immense weight of fire stopped them in their tracks as they strove to move up the beach, and no gunfire from the sea could bring them aid. With their Battalion Commander twice wounded and forced out of action, their Second-in-Command soon killed, there was nothing for it but to abandon the direct approach. Moving east the left flanking Companies of the Battalion gained les Roquettes, an objective of the 1st Dorsets on their left, and then swung right handed, seized Asnelles-sur-mer, and prepared to assault the le Hamel sanatorium. But it was afternoon before the sanatorium, resisting all infantry attacks, finally caved in to

143

Clear of the village, the perimeter widens

The casualties wait for evacuation

Counterattack

the devastating 'dustbins' of a Petard, not the least of Hobart's 'specials'.

Meanwhile the 1st Dorsets, out of reach of the le Hamel guns, had stormed up and over the beach covered by the guns of the flails and AVRE's, and had swung right handed to gain the slight rise south of Arromanches.

On the beach of la Rivière the 5th Battalion of the East Yorkshire Regiment and the 6th Battalion, the Green Howards, leading the assault of the 69th Brigade, were in no doubt about the value of the armour. From the first infantry and armour, greatly aided by close support fire from gun craft, stormed the beach defences in complete co-ordination, and fought a tight battle through the streets, eliminating 88's and pillboxes, cutting out the enemy like a canker, and moving inland. Things had been bad, but not bad enough to curb their first impetus on landing, and if men could hurl themselves over the first obstacle of the beach they must win. There was no other place to stop them but in the shallows and on the beaches.

By eleven o'clock seven lanes had been cleared on 'Gold' beach, the DD tanks were moving fast inland, and with them the 56th and 151st Brigades, carving out the centre, keeping the enemy off balance at all costs. Long before the le Hamel sanatorium had fallen the bridgehead was three miles in depth, the 56th Brigade was going well, astride the la Rivière-Bayeux road, the 151st, on its left, racing for the high ground, and beyond into the

Below: **Prisoners brought in by 13th/ 18thHussars.**

Seulles Valley, while left again the 69th pressed on for Creuilly. Even the right flank, delayed at le Hamel, had cut the Arromanches-Bayeux road, while the 47th Royal Marine Commando was working round to assault Port-en-Bessin.

The Commando had outstripped them all. The men had had a rough passage, and coming in to land west of le Hamel they had come under fire from the cliffs, and lost four out of their fourteen assault craft. Finally, forced eastward, they had run in east of the le Hamel position, hoping to find the way cleared ahead. It wasn't. They had had to fight their way through the coastal villages, each man humping 88 pounds of equipment, and covering ten miles by early afternoon. By the time the 231st Brigade began to ease their sense of isolation they were occupying the high ground south of Port-en-Bessin. No men on their feet had done more; very few had done half as much.

By the time the Canadians stormed ashore with two Brigades up astride the Seulles estuary, and raced for the

sea walls, the rising tide had reduced the gauntlet of the beaches to as little as one hundred yards at the narrowest point, and the battles of the beaches on the flanks were already from one to two hours old. The Canadians had no intention of being left behind.

The Canadian 7th Brigade, the Royal Winnipeg Regiment and the Regina Rifles leading, came in on the right, west of the Seulles river, beating the Canadian 8th Brigade to the beach by a minute or two. With them were eight, possibly ten, DD tanks manned by the Canadian 1st Hussars. The tanks had taken to the water eight hundred yards out, threatened by the turbulent sea, in constant danger of swamping, threading their ways through a maze of scantlings jutting out of the water like the stumps of some petrified forest and, plastering the enemy strong points point blank as they crawled out of the surf with the spume pouring from their grey hulls, down over their ridiculous skirts. If anyone had an eye for farce at such an hour, they might have seemed like some absurd old sea animals paddling.

On the left, the Queen's Own Regiment of Canada and The North Shore Regiment led the Canadian 8th Brigade without armour, and raced for the sea wall, the heavy machine guns of the enemy cutting swathes out of the Queen's Own in the thirty seconds or so it took them to reach the shelter of the wall. The landing craft carrying the assault armour of the Engineers were still battling with the heavy seas and the obstacles, and the DD tanks were coming in to land dry-shod when the spearhead infantry were well away, blasting the enemy out of Courseulles and Bernières, and pressing on. When the Regiment de la Chaudière came in fifteen minutes later there was scarcely a shot.

On this morning of the 6th June, when there were still a few tattered shreds of the heroic in the threadbare garment of human combat, at half-past eight o'clock, one hour late, the Canadian Battalions were borne in on a rough sea driven by the wind which flung them on to the beaches, and in one bound across them. The dangerous reefs and rocks of that narrow coast forced the assault craft to wait for the tide, and when at last they were clear of the reefs the larger craft had to charge the obstacles, hoping for the best, while the small craft strove to swerve and weave through tangles of angle iron and stakes. At one point twenty out of twenty-four assault craft blew up, and men struggled for the shore with the splinters of their landing craft falling from the skies about their ears. According to the record, 'chunks of debris rose a hundred feet in the air and troops, now hugging the shelter of a breakwater, were peppered with pieces of wood.'

Driven by the wind, the rapidly rising tide piling up the heavy surf, the helmsmen of the assault craft could only hang on and pray. The first three craft coming in on the Canadian left blew up, but their entire complement, save two killed, struggled out of the debris and water to make the beach and fight.

There were many brave men manning the landing craft all along the line from 'Sword' to 'Utah', men

Below: **The cost**

fighting lone battles against outbreaks of fire and exploding ammunition, one man at least, a man named Jones, saving wounded from drowning in a flooded hold and amputating two horribly mangled legs. He was no doctor, merely a 'sick-berth attendant', but he did the job. And there were scores of 'Joneses' at sea that day off the beaches, but none had a struggle to compare with that of the men who carried the Canadians ashore on 'Juno', and none had troops more worthy the carrying.

The LCOCU – landing craft obstacle clearance units – of the Naval demolition teams, and the beach units, striving to sort out the horrible muddle of mined obstacles, machines and men, fought like demons, and were under shell fire from enemy corps and divisional artillery long after the last mortar, machine gun and '88 of the beach defences, even the last sniper, had been silenced. Bulldozers not only bulldozed debris out of the way, but bulldozed beached craft back into the sea, giving them a start on the way back.

When the Engineer assault armour of the 22nd Dragoons and the 26th Assault Squadron, Royal Engineers, reached the beach on the Canadian 7th Brigade front, the DD tanks which had landed with the infantry, had settled the score with the worst of the enemy strong points mounting the 75-mm guns and the heavy mortars and machine guns, but there was plenty of mortar and automatic fire coming in from a bit further back. The flails were urgently needed to carve clear roads through to the exits for the mass of armour and vehicles building-up, and the Petards and bridging tanks lumbered up behind them, to keep the infantry going at high pressure.

East of the Seulles the going was good, and on both sides of the river the flails had opened the exits before half-past nine, the fascines and bridging tanks had bridged the worst of the craters and culverts, and opened the sluices of the Seulles to drain a crater as large as a village pond and twice as deep.

On the left at Bernières, flails and Petards had smashed exits through the twelve foot high sea wall, and cleared lanes and laterals well in time to work in with the infantry against the pill-boxes and strong points. Before noon on the right flank the flails were advancing inland under Command of the Canadian 2nd Armoured Brigade.

Twelve lanes were cleared that day on the 'Juno' beaches by Hobart's armour, and the exits linked right through to join the Brigade fronts. The DD tanks, beaching dry shod an hour behind the infantry, were swiftly off the beach, adding their fire-power to the men storming on inland to keep the enemy off balance and not giving him a chance to form a second line. By late afternoon the Canadian 7th Brigade was challenging the 69th Brigade of '50 Div' for the lead, its armoured patrols probing for the main Bayeux-Caen road at Bretteville, while on the left, the Canadian 9th Brigade, breaking loose from the chaos and confusion on the beach, was through the 8th Brigade, and going fast astride the Courseulles road to Caen.

The centre bridgehead from Langrune to Arromanches was solid, twelve miles wide and growing deeper every hour. The bottle neck was behind, in the congestion of the narrow beach, the struggle of armour, vehicles and men, to break loose from the appalling traffic jams. And on the right, there was the growing awareness of an ominous gap, the dangerous toe-hold of 'Omaha', inching slowly off the beach, its progress measured in yards.

Whatever happened the enemy reserves must be prevented from reaching 'Omaha', and it was this above all which made Dempsey pause, ready to reach out a helping hand, holding back his armour.

Canadian troops breaking clear of the beaches

The end of the day

Field Marshal Rommel had been right about the first twenty-four hours: they would be decisive. He had made repeated efforts to move the 12th SS Panzer and the Panzer Lehr Divisions on a line St Lô – Carentan. Had these Divisions been there the 'Omaha' beachhead must have been smashed; even had Rommel himself been there on the day, able perhaps to rouse Hitler out of his early morning dreams, it might not have been too late. It was too late when Hitler held his afternoon conference, and released the 12th SS Panzer Division.

All that could be done against the Allied Air and Seaborne assaults had been done by the forces immediately available. Feuchtinger, Commanding the 21st Panzer Division, the only counter-attacking force within reach, had reacted swiftly against the British Airborne landings on the Orne, according to his standing orders. But at once there followed a long period of uncertainty, due partly to a breakdown in communications. When at last the Division was put under Command of the 84th Corps, General Marcks, the Corps Commander, was right in his appreciation that the British 3rd Division was the more potent threat, and that Caen must be at once powerfully screened. Nevertheless, too much time had been wasted, and he might have done better to commit the Division against the Airborne bridgehead. Had that been done the great glider-borne force might have arrived to a terrible welcome.

As it was, Feuchtinger could not disengage his Infantry Battalions from the British, nor his anti-tank guns from the German 716th Division. He had been shot away from the Périers Ridge by British guns when he might have shot the British armour out of the way with his own guns – if he had any.

But 21st Panzer Division did very well. Had they not taken fright at the impressive spectacle of 250 air-tugs, towing their gliders like trains over the coast, as though they rode through some great terminus in the sky, and the evening sky black with the fighter escorts, his battle group, powerfully and swiftly reinforced, might have disrupted the British right flank on 'Sword' beach, and driven a dangerous wedge between the British and Canadians, down to the sea.

There was no second chance.

But I don't believe that the 21st Panzer could have prevailed, even the first time. The dice were too heavily loaded against the Germans. Air power had done its work, sealing off the battlefield, holding the ring, denying mobility to the reserves. Of the eleven thousand-plus sorties flown by the Allied Air Forces on the 6th June, not one single aircraft was lost to the Luftwaffe. Air superiority, it has been estimated by some staff authorities, multiplies superiority on the ground by three. On 'D day', Allied air power was overwhelming, and

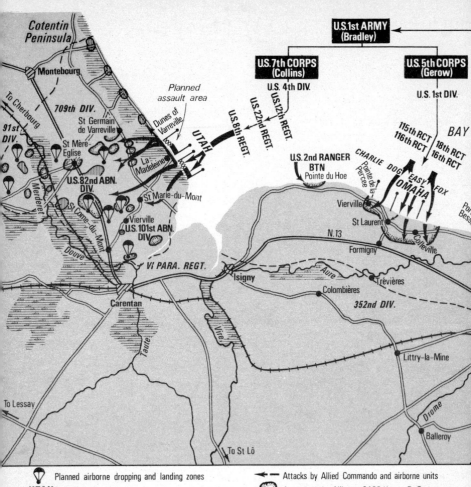

Cotentin Peninsula

To Cherbourg

Montebourg

709th DIV.

91st DIV.

St Germain de Varreville

St Mère Eglise

Dunes of Varreville

Planned assault area

UTAH

U.S. 8th REGT.

U.S.12th REGT.

U.S.22nd REGT.

La Madeleine

U.S.82nd ABN. DIV.

St Marie-du-Mont

St Come-du-Mont

Vierville

U.S.101st ABN. DIV.

VI PARA. REGT.

Merderet

Douve

Carentan

Taute

Vire

To Lessay

To St Lô

U.S.1st ARMY (Bradley)

U.S. 7th CORPS (Collins)

U.S. 4th DIV.

U.S. 5th CORPS (Gerow)

U.S. 1st DIV.

115th RCT
116th RCT

18th RCT
16th RCT

BAY

CHARLIE DOG

EASY FOX

OMAHA

U.S. 2nd RANGER BTN
Pointe du Hoe

Pointe de la Percée

Vierville

St Laurent

Colleville

Port Bess...

N. 13

Formigny

Isigny

Colombières

Trévières

Aure

352nd DIV.

Littry-la-Mine

Drome

Balleroy

Planned airborne dropping and landing zones

UTAH Assault areas

xxx Green Beach. Red Beach

First Allied assault waves

Attacks by Allied Commando and airborne units

Areas held by Allies at 2400 Hrs on D-Day

Line of planned Allied beach head at 2400 Hrs on D-Day

RCT Regimental Combat Team

decisive.

The pattern of the Battle for Normandy was beginning to set at the end of the first day, with the British and Canadians held and holding the entire enemy reserve, and the Americans exploiting the open flank. If – if that right flank could have been smashed at the outset, vulnerable, almost defenceless, on the long beach of 'Omaha', then a terrible, nagging battle of attrition might have gone on and on and on, the British bridgehead virtually sealed off. But the 6th Airborne, and then the British 3rd

Division, and then the Canadian 3rd Division, had made that 'if' impossible. General Bradley may have feared a German counter-attack, but General Kraiss, Commanding the German 352nd Division, knew that it was impossible.

And the maintenance of an 'open right flank' was essential to Allied victory. That was the point and purpose of General Montgomery's strategy, and by the end of the day he knew that he would win.

Meanwhile, by taking a chance, von Rundstedt had dared to move a power-

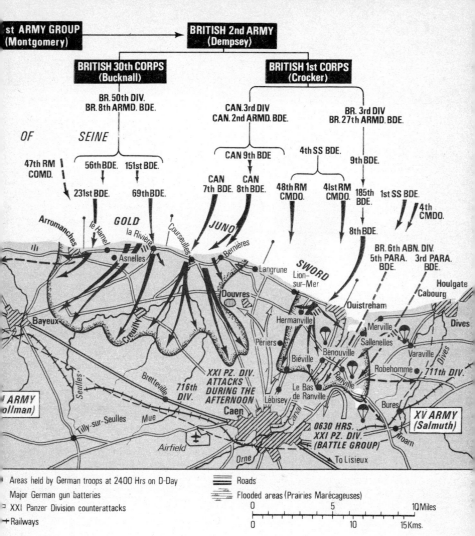

ful force of the 12th SS Panzer Division to Lisieux, and as soon as the release order came through from the High Command, this group, under Kurt Mey-er, was ordered at once to the battlefield. By midnight, constantly harassed and desperately short of petrol it reached Evrecy, nine miles south-west of Caen to find its petrol dumps a burned-out ruin. When it was able to move it had to counter a powerful Canadian threat, for it was opposite the line of advance from 'Juno' beach. Thereafter, the British and Canadian 3rd Divisions absorbed its offensive power, and severely taxed its defensive strength.

The Panzer Lehr Division was nowhere near the battlefield on 'D day'; or the day after.

'As a result of the "D day" operations a foothold has been gained on the Continent of Europe', General Montgomery was able to report.

For General Bradley, Commanding the US 1st Army, it must have been a night of grave anxieties, even – but there is no evidence – of some self-questioning. For General Dempsey, commanding the British 2nd Army,

there was cause for some satisfaction, but not for jubilation. Dempsey, of whom very little has ever been written, is a good strategist and a sound tactician, in my view one of the finest soldiers of the Second World War, distinguished then, as now, by his dignified silence. He confined himself absolutely, and with a remarkable devotion, to his work of soldiering.

On that night of the 6th June, Dempsey knew that his army had done enough. It was a good army, perhaps the last real 'army' Britain would ever produce.

The first of the landing craft, turning about, had reached the hards of England, the small ports, the estuaries, in the afternoon, swiftly replenishing ammunition, stores, men, cleaning and greasing the guns, setting forth a second time through the great maze of shipping. Through all the day and night the Mulberry tows were breaking loose, the tugs fighting scores of desperate battles with hawsers, winches and chains, clawing at the huge unwieldy objects they sought to drag through the seas. 40 per cent of the 'Whale' roadway units broke away and were lost. But it would go on, and on. There would be enough.

To the battalion, company and platoon commanders, in the forward positions, each with his small piece of the puzzle, it seemed pretty dicey. They knew only that they were 'there'. To the armoured patrols probing into Bayeux, and the Caen-Bayeux road, and drawing back, too thin on the ground, it was all 'Dragon' country. The Canadian left at Anisy, six miles in from the beach, lay upon 'nothing', an empty gulf in the darkness between them and the Shropshires at Biéville. But the gulf was not empty, rumbling with Feuchtinger's armour. And Caen, out of reach, three miles, a million miles, away.

The British 6th Airborne, reinforced by their Air Landing Brigade, their artillery, all their heavy equipment, felt strong and confident. They were trained to be out on their own. They held a good bridgehead, and fortified by success, conscious of their strength rather than their weakness, they faced the long night, which was already their second night, with high hearts. Their light tanks, coming out of the gliders under their own power, tangled hopelessly in the cords and debris of parachutes, sprockets jammed tight, did not dismay them.

But the Commandos were having rugged times. Cabourg refused to fall. At Sallenelles on the left, in the three-mile gap between 'Sword' and 'Juno', and in the chasm between 'Gold' and 'Omaha', there was no rest.

It was a strange day and a strange night both on and off the British and Canadian beachheads. Men clung marooned to obstacles and debris, on rocks, on the tops of drowned vehicles, while naval small craft, DUKWS and outboard motors, buzzed and weaved about their business, impervious to croaking cries for help, and to the full-blooded curses of frustrated, angry, frightened men. Many of those picked up by craft on the 'turn-about' were carried straight back to England whether they liked it or not, the individualists among them to 'stow away' on the first craft back, others to go slowly through 'military channels'. Three men stood with their heads and shoulders just out of the water, like giants, for the water was fifteen feet deep. The ramp of the landing craft had gone down, 'Off you go, keep moving'! And off they went into deep water. Up went the ramp. In went the ship. No backward look. 'Statistics, mate. Unavoidable error'.

There were a good many men wandering about for days in Normandy trying to find their units. Mostly they did.

Others on that first afternoon and evening, the ordeals of seasickness and the beaches behind them, lay in the lush grasses of meadows, and wrote about 'butterflies' and 'bird song', which seemed the oddest things of all in the day. On 'Sword' the pipers played 'Blue Bonnets' as the 9th Brigade of the 3rd Division came in, and the strains went with the Scots, forward.

The smoke rose in grey wisps from the burned-out houses lining the battered sea fronts from Ouistreham to Arromanches, and in the midst of the monstrous chaos of the beaches, in the jungles of shattered craft, tank tracks, wheels, and tortured iron and steel, the bodies of men lay under gas capes awaiting burial.

Several thousand men wrote home. They lay in basements, in the backs of trucks, under trucks, in slit trenches, in enemy dug-outs. Field kitchens cooked. 'Fatigue parties' dug latrines. All the normal human functions were 'taken care of' in the midst of the greatest seaborne assault the world had ever known.

Civilians stood, mostly bewildered, outside their doors, dull eyed at the rivers of men and machines filling the narrow ways, not reacting very much any more, drained dry.

Morale was high. To most of those not 'in contact', and not 'fighting' – and very few are ever 'in contact' doing any fighting – it seemed an anti-climax. One man called it 'a crashing anti-climax'. In a sense it was an anti-climax not to be dead, after so much waiting, training, thinking, and expecting 'God knew what'.

Some thought that the French were warm and friendly, others that they were suspicious and unfriendly, still others that they were indifferent. Many were startled by the extreme youth, or age, of the captured enemy and inclined to believe that it was going to be, what they called in those days, 'a piece of cake'. But the men who had charged the strong points, and gone into cellars behind grenades knew better. The German 716th Division had been cut to pieces, but its isolated 'bits' fought on.

The men, above all, who felt themselves to be 'out on a limb' that night were the US 82nd Airborne, holding on in St Mère-Eglise, and with the 101st in scores of tiny 'pockets', wondering when 'Howell Force', their small seaborne 'attachment' was going to catch up. They didn't realise – and could not – that all their small bits and pieces would presently come together and give a much greater length and breadth to the 'Utah' bridgehead than it looked.

'Howell Force' had tried hard. They spent the night, unhappily, at Les Forges, frustrated in their attempts to get through, and watching the C47's coming in, many of their gliders going straight into the arms of the enemy. The enemy held a ridge screening St Mère-Eglise, and the 3rd

Battalion, having a go at them, had called for artillery support without any luck.

But the 'Utah' bridgehead was sound. The entire 4th Division was on shore well before midnight, and much more besides, 20,000 men and 1,700 vehicles in round figures. The two leading regiments had lost twelve men killed between them. General Collins was far more worried about the possible actions – or lack of actions – of Admiral Moon, than about the bridgehead. The General wanted to go on shore, but he dared not leave the *Bayfield*. The Admiral, worrying about his 'losses', wanted to suspend landing operations through the night, and the General had 'to hold down

Admiral Moon', as Bradley put it.

General Gerow, commanding the US V Corps, with no such sea cares, but with plenty on shore, had set up his Command Post on the bluffs of that desolate stretch of coast. There were 'no rear areas on "Omaha",' that night according to the record, no comfort, no feeling of security. Enemy pockets were still firing from beach positions, sniping all night, and all through the next day. Barely 100 tons of supplies had come on shore all day, the men, weary, hungry, hanging on grimly behind Vierville, St Laurent and Colleville, were short of ammunition, sleep, short of most things. But they had found their hearts.

At the deepest point the penetration

on 'Omaha' was not much more than 1,500 yards, and there wasn't 'a line', not even the planned 'Beach Maintenance Line'. The American destroyers had closed the beach, raging up and down like wolves, engaging the enemy strong points at a thousand yards. And the men of the 1st Division who had thought, if they had thought anything at all, that they would never stand up again, had found the strength to follow men like Colonel Taylor and Brigadier-General Cota, and a handful of others off the beach. It was a miracle that they had gained a foothold, but they had. Men without armour. It was going to take them several days to catch up, and the counter-attack they feared would not come, because

German trenches deserted even by the victors

it could not.

The thoughts of everyone who knew anything about it, from General Eisenhower downwards, and not least the thoughts of General Montgomery and General Dempsey, were with the US V Corps for a week, willing them on.

Forrest Pogue wrote: 'On the central front concentric drives by US and British forces by 8th June, had closed the initial gap at the Drôme river between V and 30 British Corps. The V Corps then pushed through the *bocage* country to within a few miles of St Lô before grinding to a halt in the face of stiffening enemy defence and increasing terrain obstacles'.

In a further paragraph, Pogue comments; 'The Germans, considering Caen the gateway to Paris, massed their reserves to defend it and stopped the British short of the city'.

The US 1st Division had its beach-head ordeal on the beach. They had broken the crust, and the crust had broken itself on them. For a week it was clear ahead.

The enigma of General Bradley remains.

The Supreme Commander's report states:

'Apart from the factor of tactical surprise, the comparatively light casualties which we sustained on all beaches, except "Omaha", were in large measure due to the success of the novel mechanical contrivances which we employed and to the staggering moral and material effect of the mass of armour landed in the leading waves of the assault. It is doubtful if the assault forces could have firmly established themselves without the assistance of these weapons'.

No one may ever know what General Bradley thought about it. Why had he refused the flails, the Petards, and all the rest of Hobart's armour?

Chester Wilmot believed that it was Bradley's contempt for British 'under confidence and over-insurance'. He wasn't 'scraping the bottom of the barrel' for men, as the British were – and the Germans. So far as Bradley was concerned both British and Germans were finished, as indeed they were.

'Analysis makes it clear that the American troops paid dearly for their higher commanders' hesitation to accept Montgomery's earlier offer to give them a share of Hobart's specialised armour'.

Liddell Hart goes on to point out that this was the more remarkable because the flails were fitted to Sherman tanks 'so that no problem of adaptation arose'.

It may be that Bradley's acute anglophobia had found a focus on General Montgomery. But whatever it was the Americans paid the reckoning on 'D day' at 'Omaha' beach.

But on the night of the 6th June, all that was a long way off. What concerned the Regimental and Battalion Commanders was to get their Units well in hand, and strive with all speed to gain the 'D day' objectives.

The cost of the day in killed was not more than 2,500 men, 1,000 of them on 'Omaha'. At Towton Field, on the 29th March, 1461, 33,000 men perished by the sword and were buried there. Nearly 20,000 British troops were killed on the first day of the Battle of the Somme in 1916. Few facts underline the end of the long story of war more strongly, and mark the beginning of something new, infinitely terrible and shocking to the very soul of mankind. War had become a battle of machines against machines. Tens of thousands of tons of explosive, of copper, tungsten, bronze, iron, steel, bombs, bricks, mortar, concrete, guns, tanks, vehicles, ships, all 'blown to smithereens'. Bridges, railways, dumps, factories, whole towns, flattened to rubble, a war for bulldozers.

And presently the men controlling the bombers sensed their power, making it almost impossible for men on their feet to get through. It will be an unhappy day for the world when men on their feet cannot get through.

Eisenhower; D plus 1. His plan had succeeded

Bibliography

By Air To Battle: The Official Account of the British 1st and 6th Airborne Divisions (HMSO London)
The Battle for Normandy E Belfied and H Essame (Batsford)
Biennial Report of the Chief-of-Staff to the US Army, (1st July, 1943-30 June, 1945) to the Secretary of War
A Soldier's Story Gen Omar Bradley (Eyre & Spottiswood)
The Second World War Vols. 3, 4 and 5 Sir Winston Churchill (Cassell)
Operation Neptune Com Kenneth Edwards (Collins)
Grand Strategy Vol. 5 John Ehrman (HMSO London)
Crusade in Europe Dwight D Eisenhower (Heinemann)
Victory in the West, Vol. 1 L F Ellis (HMSO London)
Panzer Leader Heinz Guderian (Michael Joseph)
Cross-Channel Attack Gordon A Harrison (Dept. of the Army, Washington)
Air Operations by the Allied Expeditionary Force in N W Europe, 15 November, 1943-30 September, 1944 Air Chief-Marshal Sir Trafford Leigh-Mallory (4th supplement to *London Gazette*, 31 Dec. 1946)
The Tanks, Vol. 2. The Other Side of the Hill Capt. Sir Basil Liddell Hart (Cassell)
Armoured Crusader Kenneth Macksey (Hutchinson)
Memoirs F-M Montgomery of Alamein (Collins) *Normandy to the Baltic* F-M Montgomery of Alamein (Hutchinson)
Operations in North-West Europe from June 6th, 1944-May 5th, 1945 F-M Montgomery of Alamein (*London Gazette* Supplement, Sept. 3, 1946)
Overture to Overlord St.-Gen. Sir Frederick Morgan (Hodder & Stoughton)
The Supreme Command Forrest C Pogue (Dept. of the Army, Washington)
The Assault Phase of the Normandy Landings Adm. Sir Betram Ramsay (*London Gazette* supplement, Dec. 31, 1946)
Report by the Supreme Commander to the Combined Chiefs-of-Staff on the Operations in Europe of the Allied Expeditionary Force
We Defended Normandy Hans Speidel (Jenkins)
Utah Beach to Cherbourg, Omaha Beach-Head (American Forces in Action series, Historical Division, Washington)
Above Us the Waves C E T Warren and James Benson (Harrap)
The Struggle for Europe Chester Wilmot (Collins)